Tl

of the

Abbot Printers

Kings Langley Hertfordshire

England

Adrian Hodges

Published by Rins Publishing.

ABBOT

KINGS LANGLEY, HERTFORDSHIRE.

Telephone No:
KINGS LANGLEY 2274 (5 lines)

This is a brief history of the Abbot (Kings Langley) Ltd. Included are most of the main events that have influenced the company's advancement throughout the years. Please note that while the publisher has taken care to be as accurate as possible, no liability accepted under any circumstances whatsoever, should any of the contents be incorrect.

 This book was researched and compiled by Adrian Hodges.

Every attempt has been made by the publisher to secure the appropriate permission for the materials reproduced in this book. If there has been any oversight we will be happy to rectify thc oversight and will be pleased to make the necessary and reasonable arrangements at the first opportunity.

Printed and bound in Great Britain by Gemini Print Services Ltd.

ABBOT

KINGS LANGLEY, HERTFORDSHIRE.

Telephone No:
KINGS LANGLEY 2274 (5 lines)

ACKNOWLEDGMENTS

The Author would like to thank the following people and organisations for their assistance, memories, and loan of photographs etc., during this research of the history of the Abbot (Kings Langley) Ltd.

Alasdair Browne
Judy Bartlett
Dinah Chaffin
Steve Cooke
Tom Coster
Eva Davis
Roy Fuller
Kathleen Gibson
Peter Hodges
Audrey Hodges
Lee Long
Charlie Parfitt
Mick Reynolds
Jack Vickery

Apsley Paper Trail, Hemel Hempstead, Hertfordshire, UK.
Bartlett History Museum, Bartlett, IL, USA.
Kings Langley Local History & Museum Society.

Contents

Abbot (Kings Langley) Ltd

The Bartlett History

The Bartlett family founded and ran the Abbot Printing Company in Kings Langley, Hertfordshire for many years. The name Bartlett in England can be traced back to the eleventh century. The name derived from one of thousands of names brought to this country, following the Norman Conquest in 1066. Prior to this invasion, living in Lisieux, France, was Adam de Berthelot (Bartlett), a minor nobleman. Adam was the personal assistant to Guido de Brionne, a Norman Knight. They both came to England during the Norman invasion, which began on October 14, 1066. Land taken from the Anglo-Saxon owners was granted to officers, of this triumphant Norman Conquest. In Stopham, Sussex, the Ford family owned a large estate. This estate was awarded to Guido de Brionne and a part to Adam de Barthelot. The name de Brionne later became de Bryan or Brian, he then became known as Brian de Stopham. Berthelot was being spelled variously as Berthelot, Barttlelot, Bartelot and Bartlett. By the fourteenth century the Stopham family, were reduced to a daughter, she married John Bartlett, who then became the owner of the whole estate. It is most likely that, all persons in this country named Bartlett are of Norman ancestry. However, our story will start in the early 1600s, some five-hundred and fifty years, after this Norman invasion.

That time in England was marked by political and religious unrest. Families began to migrate abroad in large numbers. Faced with persecution and starvation at home, the open frontiers and less oppressive social environment of the New World looked exciting to many people. Captain John Smith, who made a famous map of this New World probably, influenced many by circulating copies of the map, along with a list of opportunities, which this new country offered to the nobility, and gentry of the southern counties in England. Among the migrants were many young men who were attracted by the love of adventure and the desire to make their fortune. Robert Bartlett, who was born on May 27, 1601, in Northampton, England, decided to make his way to North America. He embarked on the ship 'Anne' in 1623, and found himself one of a large and pleasant company, many of whom had similar aims to his own. On this long voyage of ninety days, he met a young girl, Mary Warren. Mary was travelling with her three sisters and her mother Elizabeth. The family was going to meet Richard Warren, Mary's father. He had made the journey to New England on the ship 'Mayflower'. The Mayflower reached America, in December 1620, and founded Plymouth, New England.

The ship 'Anne' reached the shores of Plymouth, Massachusetts in July 1623. Having on board besides the general, those who paid their own expenses for the voyage. This entitled them to be assigned some land. Robert Bartlett, the first Bartlett to settle in America, was one of those. On his arrival, he was granted an acre of land alongside the Eel River, Manomet, Plymouth County. Robert, continued courting Mary Warren, and they were married on May 22, 1627. As a wedding gift, Mrs Warren presented Robert with a further plot of land. The couple had twelve children together. Around 1639 the family moved some 50 miles (80 kilometres) north to Cambridge, Massachusetts. Robert worked as a cooper, a person skilled in making and repairing casks, barrels, etc.

Joseph Bartlett, the ninth child of Robert and Mary, was born in Cambridge, Massachusetts on February 15, 1646. Joseph became a shoemaker, and at the age twenty he met and fell in love with a local girl, Mary Waite, they married, two years later on October 27, 1668. By 1672 they had moved a few miles southwest to an area that would later be named Newton, Massachusetts. Newton is approximately 8 miles (13 kilometres) west of Boston, Massachusetts.

The early settlers in Newton were forced to struggle with the unpleasant and vigorous climate and a hard stony soil. They were few in number, surrounded, for a time, by Native American Indians who helped and taught them to survive the seasons, how to hunt and plant native food. The settlers created all the conveniences of living, they built their own homes, laid their roads, and bridges were thrown across the brooks and the river. The forests were changed into fruitful fields. They worked hard over many years to achieve the tasks, they had set themselves, and most accomplished what they undertook.

Joseph and Mary had six children together. However, things did not always run smoothly, as he lost his shoemaking business, and later Joseph was convicted of uncivil behaviour and rudeness toward his wife and family. His problems may have stemmed from a land dispute with his neighbour, Hugh Clark. While Joseph was building his house, John Clark, his neighbour's son, pulled down Joseph's barn and took away the timber. The courts finally resolved the dispute at first in Josephs favour, but later he lost all on appeal. By 1675, his house had been built on the north side of the hill, which included four acres of land. Joseph remained living in Newton until he died in December 1702.

Joseph's descendants continued to live in the Massachusetts area until his great-great-great grandson, Luther Pierce Bartlett, at the age of 25 made his way some 900 miles west, to Michigan. A year later Luther moved to Cook County, Illinois, and settled about 36 miles (58 kilometres) northwest of Chicago. Luther was the grandson of Adoniram Bartlett. Adoniram was a much-respected citizen, in his hometown of West Brookfield, Massachusetts, where he filled many offices of public trust. He was known for his integrity and power of reasoning. He was also a religious man and a lifelong Democrat. Luther and his younger brother, Lyman, bought 320 acres of farmland on arriving in Cook County and an additional 345 acres in 1844. Luther first tried his hand at sheep farming but abandoned this when the price of wool declined. He then turned to planting wheat, which proved a little more beneficial. Luther married Sophia, who had also moved with her parents from Luther's hometown of Conway in Franklin County, Massachusetts. They had thirteen children, the twelfth of whom Ira Albro Bartlett was born on December 3, 1861.

In 1873, many a town in America survived in accordance with its proximity to a railway line. Colonel Roselle M. Hough, president of the Chicago & Pacific Railroad, began building a rail route west to Elgin, Illinois, to challenge the Chicago and North-western Railway. People, who donated land for stations, were given the opportunity to name the villages that were created. Luther Bartlett donated 40-acres of woodland, the source of the family's timber and firewood, and named the village 'Bartlett'.

Station at Bartlett Illinois USA.
Image from the collection of the Bartlett History Museum, Bartlett, IL, USA.

The Village of Bartlett got its official start on February 11, 1891, when the petition for incorporation was filed in Springfield, Illinois. Presiding over the petition was Cook

County Judge Frank Scales, who was the husband of the Bartlett's daughter, Carrie. During the late 1800s, daily life in Bartlett centred on its train station, which was a constant bustle of people and goods heading to and from Chicago. Bartlett had just 716 residents in 1950, and resisted residential growth until the mid-1970s, when planning permission was approved to develop 540 acres south of the village. In the 1980s and 1990s, Bartlett saw even more expansion. The population again soared from 19,373 in 1990 to 36,706 in 2000. By 2010, the Village of Bartlett had a total area of 15 square miles (39 square kilometres), and the population increased to over 42,000.

Sophia Bartlett

Luther's wife, Sophia, who helped to establish the village of Bartlett in 1873, played an active part in the affairs of her community in the aftermath of The Great Chicago Fire of 1871. Following a very dry summer, the fire started during the evening on Sunday, October 8, 1871, and destroyed about 3.3 square miles (9 square kilometres). More than 300 people died, and over thirty percent of the 300,000 inhabitants, were left homeless. Sophia helped to organise food parcels, which were sent to the affected areas. She worked for the causes of the Congregational Church in Bartlett, of which she was an active member for many years. She also served as president of the Ladies Guild, championing and raising funds for local needs. Early female settlers, like Sophia, helped to build the foundation for successful development and growth, which made Bartlett what it is today. Sophia Bartlett died in 1917 at the age of ninety-one.

Luther and Sophia's son, Ira Albro Bartlett, worked for the 'Swift Beef Company' in Packing-town, the centre of Chicago's infamous meatpacking industry. The conditions in some of these factories were appalling, and corruption was rife. It was alleged that the four major meatpacking companies were conspiring to gain an unfair advantage over their competitors. It's unclear what involvement Ira had, if any. However, in 1892, he was subpoenaed to appear in court, to give evidence and to name names. His employers were not keen on this happening, and offered Ira a 'golden handshake' not to appear. He accepted this offer and left the country within three days. He made his way to England with his wife, Emma, and their baby son, who was named after his father, Ira Albro Bartlett. On arriving in England Ira became deputy-manager, representing his previous firm the Swift Beef Company, in Chicago, at Smithfield market London.

Ira and Emma had two other children, a daughter, Jennie Milliken, and a son, James Scribner, both born in England. At the age of 21, Jennie married William Barnes in September 1915 and had a son, whom they named William Scribner. Named after his father and her brother. Unfortunately, James Scribner died of pneumonia in 1936, aged 41 years; he left a widow Vera J Bartlett.

Ira Albro Bartlett, (Junior), who founded the Abbot, was born on February 8, 1891 near Chicago USA. He was only a baby when he arrived in England with his family. He was living in Brixton, Surrey, when he met Mabel Franklin, whom he married on September 4, 1913. Ira was then only 22, and Mabel was 25 years old. Ira and Mabel had two boys, who were both born in London. Brian Ira Bartlett was born on June 25, 1914, and Peter Arthur Bartlett, was born on August 21, 1919. Ira became a British citizen on April 1, 1930.

Ira Bartlett, (Junior), was a relatively quiet man, you may have thought it unlikely that he would become the head of one of the most progressive companies in the stationery trade. He believed that most, if not all business problems can be boiled down into simple answers to simple questions. Although he would not admit it, Ira had a keen interest in garden design. He eventually set up in his garden a delightful miniature railway with 200 feet

Ira Bartlett Junior

(61 meters) of double track, complete with sidings, stations, tunnels, cuttings and bridges all to the correct scale. Even the telegraph posts were correctly wired throughout the whole length. He claimed that this railway was for the entertainment of his two sons, Brian and Peter. However, his wife told a different story. She insisted that he spent as much if not more time on the project than the boys. He also enjoyed walking and badminton. Ira put down a hard surface in his garden and invited members of his company's badminton club to his house during the summer months for a match.

Another of Ira's life-long hobbies was music. He played the banjo almost professionally. Ira and his wife's brother, Stanley Franklin, got together in 1910 and played banjo duets at pubs and parties. They called themselves the 'Clifford Brothers'. They played mostly for charity. Ira wrote music for the banjo and for the piano. He also played the cello extremely well, and his wife played the piano. Together with an Italian friend, Mr. de Vito, who played the violin, the trio played regularly, although they played exclusively for their own entertainment. Ira and Mr. de Vito, however, played in the local amateur orchestra and in the local amateur operatic society's, annual productions. In his middle age, Ira became a chess fanatic. In addition to playing the game, he devised chess problems for various newspapers on a regular basis.

Ira's eldest son, Brian, was educated at the Kimbolton Grammar School and began his career with the Abbot in 1930. Brian was only sixteen years old and started as a machine apprentice, working the same hours and receiving the same wages as the other trainees. His father thought that there was no better way to learn the management of business than by practical experience in the different departments. In 1935, Brian attended the London Collage of Printing and quickly gained knowledge of all of the Abbot's trades. At the age of twenty-five, he was appointed a director of the company, and he became responsible to the Board, for all of the production side, of the Abbot's business. Brian began representing the Home Counties on the executive committee of the Master Printers' Alliance in 1947. In July 1955, he became the Vice-Chairman of the Joint Labour Committee (JLC), and determined the pay and conditions for the industry. Brian became Chairman of the JLC in 1963, a position that he held for five years before retiring from the committee in 1968. Like his father, Brian, enjoyed badminton and horse riding, and he was a keen miniature railway enthusiast. He also had a miniature railway set-up in his garden.

Brian Bartlett

Brian married Dorothy May Pleasants in June 1938. They had one child, a daughter, Dinah Louise, who was born on April 30, 1946. Dorothy had trained as an architect and designed a house, which they had built in Watford, Hertfordshire. They moved into the house in April 1959. Dorothy, who had been suffering from cancer, died in 1975. In 1977, Brian married Joan Curtis, who had been a family friend for many years and was Dinah's godmother.

Dinah Bartlett started to work at the Abbot in 1964. At first, she worked on a part time basis, six months of each year at college and six months with the company. She earned a Higher National Diploma (HND) in Print at Watford Technical College, (1964-1967), where she was the first female student in the printing department. Dinah specialised in work-study and design. Her biggest fear was that, as the daughter of the managing director, she would be seen as having obtained her position in the company because of who she was rather than on merit. To counter this, she did several training courses as her role in the company increased, which included General Management, Accounting for Management, Total Quality, Auditor Training and Investors in People. She became the Assistant Company Secretary to Ron Beddall in 1985 assumed his position, together with that of a Pension Scheme Trustee, when Ron retired in 1986. At the same time, she was also made a director of the company.

Dinah Bartlett, 1966.

Dinah's only hobby as a child was her horses. She loved everything associated with them and enjoyed nothing more than being out riding her horses. Dinah married James Wilcox on April 16, 1969. They first lived in St. Leonards near Tring, Hertfordshire, where their only child, Sonia, was born on July 11, 1973. The following year, they moved to Leighton Buzzard, Bedfordshire. During the 1970s, Dinah's main hobby was archery. She spent eighteen years as Secretary of the English Field Archery Association and edited their quarterly magazine.

Dinah was selected for the English Field Archery Team in the late 1970's.

James and Dinah divorced in 1979. She married her second husband, Roy Chaffin, on April 19, 1980. At that time, Roy was in the Royal Air Force stationed at Stanbridge on the outskirts of Leighton Buzzard, Bedfordshire. He was a member of the English Field Archery Team, which is how they had met. Roy had two children, Tony and Mandy, by his first marriage. They all became a composite family. They lived briefly in Bronte Close, Aylesbury, Bedfordshire, and then moved to Linslade near Leighton Buzzard. Upon the death of Dinah's stepmother, Joan, Dinah and the family moved temporarily to Watford to look after her father Brian. Within a year, they sold their Linslade bungalow. They bought and moved into Brian's house, 'Blackwood', in Watford.

Peter Bartlett, the youngest son of Ira Bartlett, was educated at the Merchant Taylors' School, Northwood, which was an independent day school for boys, and the London School of Printing. He started at the Abbot in 1938 and was voted onto the board of directors, on February 28, 1947. Just after the war, Peter met Sammie Stewart, a war widow, who was lodging with friends in Chipperfield. Sammie was 15 years older than Peter. They married in 1946. As a child, Sammie had contracted glandular fever and was unable to have children. They adopted a son, Nikolas John. Nikolas was born in Dublin to a young Irish girl. His father was a wing commander and a friend of Sammie. The family lived in a cottage in Kings Lane, Chipperfield, Hertfordshire. Later, they moved to Frenches Farm on the outskirts of the village. Peter was a keen

Peter Bartlett

steam engine enthusiast. He bought and restored a 1928 Foster 5hp single cylinder traction engine named ‘Matilda’ with his friend, Peter Williams. They attended many shows with Matilda. Although Peter had a workshop at his home, he nevertheless regularly had new and modified parts made for his steam engines and probably those of his friends by the Abbot’s engineering department. Peter regularly commandeered Arnold Morton, who worked in the company’s garage maintaining its vehicles, to help Peter maintain and repair his traction engine.

Peter and Sammie’s adopted son, Nikolas was educated at the Ely School, Cambridgeshire. He went to work for the Abbot straight from school. Nikolas worked in most departments in the company but primarily as a paper buyer. He had an erratic career with the company, and unfortunately, he became an alcoholic. He struggled with this problem throughout his life. Nikolas met and married Susan Hobbs, and they also made their home in Chipperfield. Nikolas and Susan had two children, Jemma and Alexander.

Nikolas Bartlett

Peter divorced Sammie in 1968. He met his second wife, Judy Miller, on a skiing trip in Austria. They married in 1969. Peter and Judy moved to Hillmeads Farm, Penmans Green, Chipperfield. Sammie and Nikolas continued to stay at Frenches Farm. Peter and Judy had two daughters together, Catherine and Polly, neither of whom ever worked for the Abbot. Due to ill health, Peter reluctantly sold his traction engine ‘Matilda’ in 1990 to Geoffrey Shackle, who was the nephew of Arthur Napper. Arthur was primarily responsible in 1950, for starting the ‘Steam Preservation Movement’ as it is called today. Geoffrey Shackle later sold Matilda to Richard Wilcox of

Stoneleigh, who was a collector and Chairman of the 'Road Locomotive Society'.

His cars were another of Peter's many interests. He owned a gold and brown Porsche. He was also interested in farming and would have admitted frankly, that he would have loved to have been a farmer, if the rewards had been on par with his income from the Abbot.

Ira Bartlett thought it would be an advantage to the business if his two boys could speak a second language. As a teenager, Brian spent a year in France learning the language. Peter was sent to Vienna in Austria to learn German. Unfortunately, he had to return after six months, due to the outbreak of the Second World War. Both Brian and Peter eventually spoke their chosen languages, fluently.

Peter Bartlett and his friend Peter Williams.

Peter, Judy, Catherine & Polly.

Early Days

The Chicago meatpacking industries ran sideline businesses from the bi-products of their meat plants. They made such things as glue, dyes, perfumes and soaps. It may have been that Ira Bartlett Senior had some knowledge on these sideline businesses, which may have influenced him into buying a soap business, Pavitt & Co Ltd, based at 13 Steedman Street Walworth, Southeast London. Pavitts manufactured soap cleansing and washing powders. Ira Albro Bartlett (junior), started his working life in his father's successful soap business. At the age of twenty in 1911, he became a salesman for Manifold Printing Company, the registered offices of which were situated in West Bromwich, Staffordshire. Ira started on a salary of thirty shillings (£1.50) per week and remained with this company for nine years. With the knowledge gained while working for Manifold Printers, Ira decided to start his own business. With the help of his father, on July 22, 1920, they registered a company at the same address as the soap business, which they called Pavitt Sons and Co. Ltd. Initially, the company was a dealer in paper, twine, cord and packing materials. The initial investment was £3,000, and the first directors were Herbert Douglas Candlish and Susanna Kate Franklin. On August 3, 1920, at their very first meeting, the directors appointed John Kennedy Myers manager and Secretary of the company on a salary of £6 per week. It was also resolved at the meeting, that an account be opened at Lloyds Bank Ltd at 151 Newington Causeway S.E.1. All company cheques had to

be signed and countersigned, by Ira Bartlett Senior and Ira Bartlett Junior.

In December 1921, the Director and Chairman of Pavitt Sons & Co. Ltd. Ira Bartlett (junior) announced his desire to take a more active role in the company's management. He outlined his views on the possibility of expanding the business to include printing, binding and general stationery. He agreed to take full responsibility for the organisation and control of this new branch. It was then decided to change the company's name to Pavitt & Bartlett Ltd. This company name was registered on December 28, 1921. As the business began to increase, the directors decided to lease offices on the third floor of Metropolitan House, Charterhouse Street, E.C.1. This became the company's new registered address and the relevant authorities were informed of this change.

To expand the company further, Ira talked to Horace Young and Archibald Thomas Hutchinson of H Young & Co. Wealdstone, about merging the two businesses. The board of directors eventually agreed, and the purchase of Horace Young & Co. Ltd. took place on February 21, 1923. Thereafter, the possibility of obtaining larger premises and the question of finance in connection with building a factory were discussed. Since Archibald Hutchinson lived in Chipperfield, Hertfordshire, he suggested that a plot of land locally, on the outskirts of Kings Langley in Railway Terrace would be perfect for their needs.

Kings Langley is a historic English village in Hertfordshire, which originated during the Anglo-Saxon times. The village is situated 21 miles (34 kilometres) northwest of central London, and has a wealth of royal connections. A Royal Palace was erected as early as 1299 at the top of what is known today as Langley Hill. Unfortunately, there are no longer any remains of the palace visible above the ground, as the site is now occupied by the Rudolf Steiner School. A small display of items from the palace era, which were recovered during the excavations during the 1970s, can be seen in the school entrance hall. Building of the Kings Langley Priory, adjacent to the palace started in 1308. Part of some of these buildings from the priory site, remain in use today by the Rudolf Steiner School.

All Saints Church, Kings Langley.

The 'All Saints' church in Kings Langley was built during the fourteenth century on a site of an earlier church. King Richard II who died on February 4, 1400 was buried here. His body was later removed to Westminster Abbey, London. Edmund de Langley the first Duke of York, the son of Edward III, was born at the Royal Palace, Langley (Kings Langley). Following his death, on August 1, 1402 he was laid to rest in the Friary Church. In 1574 following a devastating fire his tomb was removed from the Priory and placed in the north end of the Chancel of the Parish Church. The tomb is still located at All Saints Church, in the village. Ancestors of Jimmy Carter, the 39th President of the United States of America (1977-1981), lived in the village, between the years 1361-1588. Today, the village has a population of almost 6,000. It has an attractive blend of timber-framed buildings ranging from the eighteenth century. Kings Langley has a thriving High Street with a good range of shops, a colourful cafe culture, serving the local community.

Ira Bartlett and Archibald Hutchinson used their savings, mortgaged their homes, and sold their personal possessions to raise the money required to build the factory in Kings Langley. Even this was not sufficient, and another director, Albert E. Macey, came to the rescue with £3,000. By May of 1923, the land had been purchased in Kings Langley. By agreement Archibald took charge of the organisation, the purchase of new machinery, and routine work associated with the new factory. This relieved Ira and Horace sufficiently to concentrate on obtaining new business. The new factory in Railway Terrace opened on November 5, 1923. Archibald was responsible for factory organisation, and all matters in connection with production. This new corrugated iron building was at first queried by passers-by as "Mission hall or Garage"?

When the company opened in Kings Langley, it laid down one main principle as the basis of its whole policy. The company would have a trade only policy. The company believed that printers and stationers could sell specially printed duplicate books quite as successfully as the big specialists that traded direct. Business continued to increase, and, by January of 1925, it became increasingly obvious that more space was required to maintain a steady growth. All agreed that a new bay should be added to the factory, and Horace Young was instructed to contact David Rowell and the Aston Construction Company for the purpose of obtaining competitive estimates.

The new bay erected, in 1925.

FIG.1.

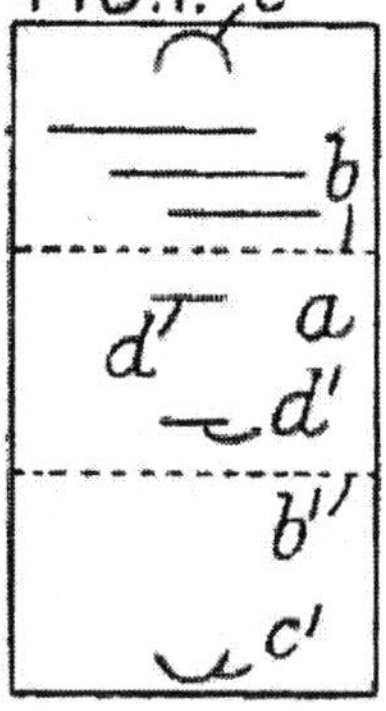

In May of 1924 Ira and Archibald applied for a patent for an improvement in fastening folded invoices and the like (see fig 1 right). The idea was for fastening folded invoices for postal transmission. The process involved folding the lower part of the sheet over the front of the central part and its tongue then inserted into slit (d). The upper part of the sheet was then folded over the back of the central part and its tongue inserted into the same slit (d). The folded item was then ready for posting.

Ira applied for additional patents. In April of 1927, he sought a patent for duplicate books with tear-out portions. The idea was for the books to have wide margins for the application of advertisements, price lists, and the like. Additional improvements were also made to advertising devices in 1936. A book page or sheet had one or more tongues cut out, by which a smaller sheet containing an advertisement could be attached to the page or sheet and folded over. It was thought that the tongues could be cut to resemble animal heads or the like. A UK patent normally lasted for twenty years, from the time of issue.

In August of 1925 some differences of opinion between Ira and Horace, became critical. One of the main points was the trade-only policy. However, Ira brought to the notice of the board of directors instances, in which it appeared that Horace had attempted on various occasions, to undermine the loyalty of Mr Hutchinson and Mr Myers to himself. Both Mr Hutchinson and Mr Myers validated these facts. Ira said: "In view of the position in which the company found itself and the need for complete freedom of action and harmonious working, I would like to put forward the following resolution: - That in view of Mr Young's conduct in wilfully endeavouring to create dissention between the other directors, by methods which have been completely discredited, he be called upon to resign from the board." This was seconded by Mr Hutchinson and passed. Horace, who voted against this resolution had no intention of resigning and requested that the board find a purchaser of his holding at a reasonable price. At the next directors meeting held on October 16, 1925, it was reported that Horace's shares in the company, had been sold to his satisfaction.

As Railway Terrace was based in the parish of Abbots Langley, they automatically started naming some of their earlier stock lines, Blue Abbot, Brown Abbot, Grey Abbot, and so on. This proved very popular with customers. Consequently, this business became known as 'The Abbot People'. This gave Ira, the idea for a little Abbot figure, whose activities would seek to brighten the pages of their advertising material. He became an amusing, likeable little fellow, representing a cheerful and happy service, which was the aim and purpose that the organisation wanted to give to

the trade. Everyone became very fond of this little character. It was rumoured that the directors of the company wore a miniature of him on a chain, around their necks.

In the summer of 1928, the will of the late Ira Albro Bartlett Senior was read. The will stated that his shares in the company would be transferred to the executors, namely his wife, Emma C Bartlett, his son, Ira Albro Bartlett, and his daughter's husband, William Barnes. The company secretary, Mr Candish, was then instructed to issue the new share certificates.

Ira Bartlett Senior

To reflect their company's type of business, on April 9, 1929, Ira, and his directors decided to change the company name from Pavitt & Bartlett Ltd. to Abbot Trade Printers Ltd. During this period the company had also decided to set up two subsidiary companies. Abbot Trade Book Company and Abbot Duplicate Book Company. The company traded under these names rather than the holding company name. The Abbot Trade Book Company started as a shop premises and showroom on January 21, 1929, at 33 New Bridge Street London EC4.

The factory, before the decorative front.

The factory was extended five times between 1924 and 1934. The two-storey extension at the rear of the building was built between 1930 and 1932. This later housed the compositors, foundry and reel-fed departments. The extension with the distinctive decorative front, designed by a local architect, Percy Previtt of Bovingdon, was erected in 1935. Some houses alongside the company had to be purchased and then demolished to make way for this extension to the front. The extension included a door from the boardroom that led into a roof garden, complete with a goldfish pond. It was thought those goldfish might have helped Ira make many executive decisions. The main lobby was large and spacious and was always kept in immaculate condition, which created a good impression to all visitors.

Demolition of houses to make way for the Abbot extensions.

A suggestion in January of 1930 by one of the company directors, Albert Macey, was for the girls of the office staff and three of the girls from the factory staff to be allowed one afternoon's absence every other month for a 'shopping day'.

This was approved, and, on Ira's, suggestion, these days were to be called 'Macey Days'.

In 1932, the recently widowed Emma Bartlett, Ira's mother, brought a Humber Snipe, a luxury four-door saloon. In 1936, Ira and his mother decided to drive across Europe to Switzerland. On route, they visited a printing exhibition/trade Fair in Belgium. There they met two fellow printers, who ran their own businesses. Gerhard Kemme, a Dutchman from Blauwe Wereld near Hilversum, Holland, and Richard Seeger from Boblingen near Stuttgart, Germany. Both had factories that were similar in size to the Abbot. They all became very good friends. In spite of loosing all contact during the war years, their friendship was quickly resumed thereafter.

Kobi Kemme, Gerhard's daughter, visited Brian and Dorothy at their home in Watford and again later with her husband, Jos van der Vorst. The young couple had five children and made many visits to Chipperfield. Their children stayed at Hillmeads Farm for a while to help perfect their English. Ralf Seeger the son of Richard Seeger, came over as a nineteen year-old and spent a year working at the Abbot. In his twenties, due to his father's early death, Ralf took over the family printing business, Seeger & Cie, in Germany.

The Abbot works were situated in the Abbots Langley Parish between the villages of Abbots Langley and Kings Langley. Although the factory had always been situated in Railway Terrace, from April of 1935 the authorities wanted to serve them from the Kings Langley Post Office, which was nearer and much larger than the post office in Abbots Langley. Prior to this change, the Abbot works had, in addition to its Abbots Langley address, a 'Box Number' address, which was adopted to overcome the difficulty that arose, because the parish and postal boundaries overlapped. Even though the factory did not move an inch, the new address became Abbot Duplicate Book Co Ltd, Abbot Works, Kings Langley, Hertfordshire. To reflect this new postal address, on June 21, 1943, the parent company name was changed again, this time to Abbot (Kings Langley) Ltd.

Business continued to increase and, by 1938, it became obvious that more room would be needed. The company then purchased Land, 200 yards south of the factory in Primrose Hill. Here, smaller factory units were built, at first to accommodate the engineering staff. A subsidiary company named Gade Engineering Co. Ltd. The company first registered, Gade Engineering as a company, on Thursday, February 2, 1939. However they did not start trading until October 1939. It was invaluable for the development of new ideas. Much of the specialised plant used over the years by the Abbot was designed and built by the Gade engineering department. The engineering department was also responsible for all maintenance and was able to ensure that breakdowns, when they occurred, were kept to a minimum to meet the demands of the Abbot's prompt delivery service. Its other duties included the maintenance and control of the company's diesel-driven generating-plant and the motor vehicles operated by the company. In addition to the engineering staff, a painter, carpenter and electrician were employed to help keep the works up to the high standards that Ira always expected. Alongside this new building was the company garage. At a later date, a petrol pump was installed for the use of company vehicles.

Abbot No. 2 works, and company garage on right.

From January 22 to March 17, 1947, snow fell every day somewhere in the UK. With the weather so cold, the snow accumulated. The temperature seldom rose more than a degree or two above freezing. Across Britain, drifts more than five metres deep blocked roads and railways. People were cut off for days. The armed services had to drop supplies by helicopter to isolated farmsteads and villages, and they helped to clear roads and railways. In certain areas, which included Kings Langley, the Ministry of Fuel and Power decided to prohibit the use of electricity, except for essential services. Therefore, it was decided to close the factory on Monday February 11, 1947. Half wages were paid to all employees during the closure. This unexpected holiday for the workforce lasted two weeks. On their return to work, none of the staff reported spending any time at the coast with their families and loved ones. At the time of this cold snap, staff received only four days paid holiday a year, two at Christmas and the other two at Easter. Staff could take a week's summer break, but this was unpaid.

As insurance against any future power cuts, in December of 1947 the Abbot installed a 55-kilowatt diesel generator, at a cost of £2,500. This generator did not have sufficient capacity to supply the factory's entire demand. With careful usage, however, it could meet 9/10ths of the electricity needed to maintain production.

Edmund Arthur Price was one of the original directors of Gade Engineering when it was first registered as a company in 1939. Eddie, as he was known, was in charge of the engineers. He was a tall, well-built, red-faced man, who wore glasses and had swept-back, black hair. Eddie liked to spend his nights drinking in a variety of establishments in the area, which probably accounted for his red face. During the evening of Friday, November 17, 1966, Eddie Price was driving back from the Hemel Hempstead area, when his car hit a wall in Lower Road, Kings Langley. In the accident, Eddie was thrown through the windscreen of his vehicle, receiving serious head and chest injuries. He was taken to hospital in Hemel Hempstead, where he was admitted into intensive care. After 24 hours, Eddie was still desperately fighting for his life. Unfortunately, the following day Eddie lost that battle. Following this tragic incident, Bertram John Martin, who was known as John Martin, took over the position as manager of Gade Engineering, under the directorship of Peter Bartlett. John Martin had started his career with the Abbot as an electrician.

At an extraordinary general meeting held on March 25, 1969, at Pavitt & Co Ltd, manufactures of soap, cleansing and washing powders, the Company Ira Bartlett's Senior had bought into on his arrival in England, was wound up voluntarily. The chairman of the company at the time of its closure was William Barnes, the husband of Ira's daughter Jennie.

Abbot stand, at a London trade fair.

Abbot Football

From the early days of the factory, there was a works football team, which, like most other teams in the area, took part in the annual Uncle's Cup competition. The Uncle's Cup is one of the oldest, local football competitions, which started as a John Dickinson departmental trophy, at Apsley Mills, Hertfordshire. Back in the late 1800s, teams from the John Dickinson Paper Mill would play inter-departmental competitions on Salmon Meadow in Apsley End, now the site of the Apsley Mill Retail Park.

Salmon Meadow Apsley End, Hertfordshire, England.
Image reproduced by kind permission of Eva Davis.

The picture above shows a view of Salmon Meadow situated alongside John Dickinson paper mill in Apsley, taken between 1914 and 1920. Salmon Meadow was originally the home ground of the Apsley Football Club, which later became the Hemel Hempstead Town Football Club. Christopher Hawkins, was the landlord of the Salmon Public House situated across the road from the Meadow, and close to St Mary's Church. Christopher 'Uncle' Hawkins, as he was known locally, enjoyed his football and would regularly wander across and watch those Dickinson inter-departmental games.

By 1897, Uncle Hawkins had suggested to the organisers that he would like to donate and present a trophy to the winners of future competitions. Consequently, in 1898, Uncle Hawkins presented the winners with a trophy, which became known as the 'Uncle's Cup'. Over the years, other local amateur works teams, including the Abbot's, were invited to join this competition. Christopher 'Uncle' Hawkins died in March of 1924, at 88 years of age. However, local firms still play for his trophy during the months of April and May each year. All proceeds from the competition are presented to a local charity.

By the early 1930s, Frank Sexton, one of the managers and Archibald Hutchinson, the managing director, were keen to see an Abbot Football Club in more serious competitions. As some of the staff already turned out for clubs, such as Kings Langley FC, they were persuaded to play for the Abbot Football Club, which intended to play in a local league and cup competitions.

In the 1932/33 season, Abbot FC started out in the fourth division of the Watford and District League. In this first season, the team was remarkably successful, finishing runners-up to the champions, Chandlers Cross, and was consequently promoted into the third division. By the end of the 1933/34 season, Abbot FC finished fourth in division three of the Watford and District league.

When this Abbot side started out, they played their home games at Home Park Meadow, Station Road, Kings Langley, which was the home ground of Kings Langley FC. By the 1934/35, season Abbot FC had joined the Herts FA league, and the team then moved to Aldridge's Farm, Kings Langley. The club secretary was Horace Luckett, who changed the team's colours from all white to red shirts and white shorts.

Abbot Team 1931/32

Back row: George Ekins, Frank Sexton, ??, George Grundy, ??, George Freeman, Harry Newton, Horace Luckett.
Middle row: ??, Tom Farmer, Roland Funnel, Harold Freeman, Harold Gibbs
Front row: Ron Walton, Edgar Spall, ??.

In February of 1935, Abbot FC played Kings Langley FC in the Apsley cup. It was an impressive performance by Abbot FC, but they eventually lost six goals to two. The Abbot team line-up that day was: George Grundy (goal); Pat White and Horace Luckett (fullbacks); Don Sears, Reg Gurney and Arthur Young (halfbacks); Cecil Sessions, Sid Briggenshaw, Roland Funnel, Richard Waterton and C. Wood (forwards).

For the 1935/36 season, Abbot FC joined the West Herts Football League and was admitted into the third division. Having no ground to play on, in November of 1935, the team withdrew from the league, although it returned the following season (1936/37) to play in division two of the West Herts League. The team was no longer based in Kings Langley but now played at Hunters Lane, Leavesden. Playing at Leavesden was not an acceptable solution to their ground problems, so it was decided not to enter a team into the West Herts League for the 1937/38 season. The Abbot Football Club played its very last league game away to the Chorleywood Football Club on Saturday, May 1, 1937, beating the home team three goals to one.

Abbot Football Club 1932/33.

Back row: Don Sears, Pocock, Edgar Spall, White.
Third row: Harry Dennett, Ron Walter, George Grundy, Alf Hobbs, ??.
Second row: Wilf Tipton, Harry Reeves, Pat White, Fred ?, Horace Luckett, Don Griffin (goal), Tom Farmer, George Allen, Harold Freeman, Arthur Young.
Front row: Arthur Parkes, Mr Albert Macey, Ira Bartlett,

The Abbot FC never returned to the senior game, but the works side was a regular competitor in the Uncles Cup competitions. In 1968, the Abbot team reached the final for the very first time playing against Honeywell Controls at Hemel Hempstead Football Club's home ground, located in Crabtree Lane. There was much celebration and preparation in the week leading up to the final.

The female Abbotonians enjoyed themselves making hats and various articles of clothing to wear at the final. The game was well supported by many Abbot fans, including the Bartlett's and most of the management. The game was an exciting affair, although there was very little between the two teams. After ninety minutes, the score was one each. Sadly during the second half of extra time, Abbot conceded a further goal and lost two goals to one. In spite of losing the Abbot supporters descended on the Steam Coach public house in Boxmoor, where a buffet had been arranged. This buffet was accompanied by large amounts of alcohol and a good selection of bawdy songs.

Uncle's Cup Final Team 1968.

Standing. Left to right: Colin Rhodes, Gerry Howe, Terry Parkins, Pete Rolph, Roy Lamb, Phil Carter, Math Darvill, Keith White (coach).

Kneeling. Left to right: Sid Howard, Roy Barter, Bill Barker, Tony Townley, Charlie Parfitt.

There continued to be plenty of support by both male and female Abbotonians for these cup games over the years. At the end of those matches, many supporters would always make their way to the Steam Coach in Boxmoor, Hemel Hempstead to celebrate or to drown their sorrows. Either way, the bar takings would dramatically increased, and there were always plenty of sore heads, the next morning.

Charlie Parfitt

In the eighties, under the management of Charlie Parfitt, the Abbot works team had some of their best performances in the Uncle's Cup. In 1986, they had a 13-0 win over Maine Engineering, a 2-0 victory against Brook Bond, and a close game with Hipgrave with the Abbot winning 5 goals to 4 after penalties. Unfortunately, they lost in the semi-final to Marpost 'A' 4-0. In 1987, Abbot reached the final for only the second time. This game was played at the Hemel Hempstead Football Club's home ground, now located at Vauxhall Road, Hemel Hempstead. On the road to the final, they beat A.M. International 4-2, Linkshore 4-0, and Dacorum Council 2-0. The final was played on May 12, 1987, and was one of the closest finals for some years.

The Abbot supporters far outnumbered the opposition's; unfortunately, they were unable to spur the team onto victory, as they eventually lost 4-1 to Hemel Hempstead Schoolmasters XI. This match was followed again by the traditional trip to the Steam Coach to reflect on the evening's game over a good few drinks.

The following year (1988), they reached the final for the third and last time, losing to Nikel Windows 2-1. Again, this game was followed by a trip to the Steam Coach to commiserate.

Uncle's Cup Final Team 1987.

Back row: Sean Byford, Kevin Culverhouse, Andy McCloud, Peter Kinchen, Martin Stankey, Ken Redgwell, Denis Fletcher. **Front row:** Steve Lacey, Neil Livermore, Chris O'Connor, Steve Hardy, Phil Stride, Barry Redgwell.

Uncle's cup, runners-up trophies. 1987 & 1988.

During the War

At the outbreak of the Second World War, those employees eligible were called-up into the armed forces, which left a small work force behind. As the war progressed, the Abbot and Gade factories were taken over by Ultra Electric Ltd. Like many other radio manufacturers, Ultra turned its production capabilities over to equipment for the war effort.

Truly, no shipyard, munitions factory or any national service could operate without the kind of books and forms that the Abbot supplied. Nevertheless, the requirements of the armed forces were a higher priority, and, at this critical time, there was no alternative but to co-operate with the government. First, the engineering department was taken over entirely by the Admiralty, the Ministry of Supply, and the Ministry of Aircraft Production. The department was considerably enlarged during the war years and produced many thousands of intricate components in a great variety.

To minimise aircraft losses, the government decided to introduce self-sealing petrol tanks. Theses were of little use unless the rest of the fuel system was treated similarly. A brilliant invention by Bernard Wilkinson of Wilkinson Rubber Linatax Ltd made this possible, and the Abbot engineers were called upon to help in this production stage. Under Mr Wilkinson's guidance, they designed and built the necessary machines for the manufacture of self-sealing fuel pipes. In all, over three million feet (915,000 meters) of aircraft piping was made at the Abbot. These were installed by the aircraft builders in many planes, including the Lancaster and the Mosquito, to help prevent leakage of fuel in the event of damage caused by enemy fire. Many young RAF lives were likely saved due to the work carried out at the Abbot factories. During this time, the Gade factory became known as the 'Pipe Factory'. Brian Bartlett was not allowed to join the regular armed forces, as his work was considered too valuable to the war effort. But he did serve in the Home Guard from August 27, 1942 until December 31, 1944. Peter Bartlett served in the Chipperfield division of the Home Guard.

The manufacture of the self-sealing fuel pipes in the Gade factory.

On May 14, 1940, the government broadcast a message asking for volunteers for the Local Defence Volunteers (LDV). On August 23, 1940, Winston Churchill changed the name from LDV to the Home Guard. The Home Guard was formed to confront the real threat of invasion. Most men who could fight were already in the forces; those left were either too young, too old or were engaged in valuable war work at home. The men who volunteered to join the Home Guard were expected to fight an invasion of elite German troops with nothing more than a collection of old shotguns and pieces of pipe with bayonets welded on the end. The government expected 150,000 men to volunteer for the Home Guard. Within the first month, over 750,000 men had volunteered, and, by the end of June 1940, the number of volunteers had increased to over a million. During the hostilities, the number of men in the Home Guard did not fall below one million. The Home Guard stood down in December of 1944 and was disbanded on December 31, 1945.

For the duration of the war, the downsized Abbot production was moved to John Dickinson's Home Park Paper Mill, Station Road, Kings Langley. The Home Park Paper Mill, become known by Abbotonians, as their No. 3 factory.

During the fuel shortages and rationing that took place at the beginning of 1943, the company decided to purchase an electric vehicle. The chassis for this vehicle was quickly obtained. Unfortunately, the company, which originally were going to fit the body, was no longer able to do so. A promise was then received from Bradshaw of Hemel Hempstead to build the body at a cost of £75. However, other quotations were obtained. Eventually, the order to build this body was placed with Bridge Motors, Hemel Hempstead. The chassis was then delivered back to them in March. The van was taxed and insured from the beginning of May. It was received back from the body builders in mid-May, 1943. Before the van could be put into service, the batteries and charging system needed to be inspected by the suppliers, who would not otherwise guarantee the life of the batteries. The company used the van successfully, on the shorter runs, until 1951.

On Saturday, December 16, 1944, a dinner function was arranged in the Abbot canteen for "B" Company of the Home Guard, 9th Battalion, which was under the command of the company's sales manager and later director H Gordon Smith. On the menu was soup with ham and beef, hot potatoes and salad, apple pie, cheese roll, and, to finish, coffee and biscuits. The toastmaster for the evening was 2nd Lt P R C Miller, who made toasts to 'The King', Honorary

Colonel of the Hertfordshire regiment, 'The Queen' and B Company of the Hertfordshire, 9th Battalion. The Dick Dudley Concert Party provided entertainment for the evening. 243 members of the Home Guard attended the evening.

During the early part of the war, on October 20, 1940, the Germans tried to bomb the railway line in Kings Langley. The Luftwaffe missed the railway and fortunately the Abbot buildings, although sadly one of the stray bombs hit 'The Griffin' public house in Water Lane, killing the landlord, Ted Carter and his dog. Ted was the only person killed by enemy action in the village during World War Two.

As the war was drawing to a close, it was anticipated that the No. 1 factory would be returned to the Abbot by the beginning of December, 1944, and that Ultra Electrics Ltd aimed to be completely out by February 28, 1945. Much work was needed to bring the stored machinery back into operation before any production could be restored at the Abbot.

After five years, eight months, and five days of massive devastation, the end of the European phase of World War Two finely arrived. Victory in Europe (VE Day) was commemorated with celebrations all around the country in recognition of the unconditional surrender of all German forces on May 7, 1945. During nearly six-years of hardship, half a million homes were destroyed, thousands of civilians had been killed and millions of lives were disrupted.

Although the casualty lists from the battlefields were lower than those in World War One, they were still appalling. The British people began to rejoice straight away. Abbotonians got together and organised an event primarily designed for the children, most of whose fathers were away in the forces. Miraculously, the ingredients for a most wonderful tea party were provided for over 200 children, who were invited to the Abbot canteen.

In the roadway along the whole frontage of the works, a model railway made by the engineers was laid down. The engine, named 'Victory Express', was electrically driven by car batteries. The children operated the engine entirely by themselves, appointing their own stationmaster, ticket collectors and signalmen. As darkness fell, a huge bonfire was lit on the banks of the lake opposite. After the dreary black-out years, this was truly magnificent.

Victory Express – overseen by Ira Bartlett.

Then came the fireworks! The expressions on the children's faces were a joy to see, as only then did the adults realise that many of them had never before seen these fiery wonders. After the fireworks, when the children had been persuaded to go to bed, a piano was produced, and the evening continued with an old-time sing-song around the fire that continued burning late into the night. At Christmas that year, the board of directors decided to pay all employees a 'Victory Bonus' of an extra week's wages. This bonus was later extended to all those members of the forces, who returned to the company's employment.

Following the end of the war in Europe, things began to return to normal. Kings Langley Village School in Church Lane asked for help toward obtaining a proofing press primarily for use in printing the school magazine and to help with the efforts of the educational training department. The company agreed to donate the full cost of the press. As the result of the interest shown in the use of the letterpress printer, it was anticipated that pupils of the school might be attracted to employment at the Abbot at a later date. It was also agreed to allow the school to have some other equipment to help with its educational needs. All agreed that Archibald Hutchinson would help with the selection of the right type of press and equipment, to suit the schools needs.

Abbot Business

In the early days, it was a small and struggling company, and paydays were not always forthcoming. The purchasing of new machinery presented a major problem for Ira Bartlett in his effort to expand production. Ira was always extremely polite to his bank manager. However, this did not guarantee a favourable response to his requests for financing. Nevertheless, the company continued to expand due to the acute business mind of Ira Bartlett (junior).

From the start, the company business comprised of the manufacture of carbon duplicating stationery, which included duplicate, triplicate and quadruplicate books of every kind, invoice books, credit books, delivery books, order books, receipt books and an extensive list of interdepartmental books. In addition the company printed catalogues, booklets, folders and brochures for their customers' individual needs.

Gordon Smith

Ira Bartlett held very strong views on advertising, claming it to be one of the most important departments in any business. For this reason, in the early days he personally handled the whole of the Abbot's extensive advertising. In 1931 Gordon Smith joined Ira's sales team. Gordon carried the flag for the Abbot in Scotland. He went on to become the sales manager in 1939 and was appointed a director of the company in 1945. Gordon eventually became a member of the exclusive '35 Club', whose members were employed by the company for 35 years or more.

Sometimes the company was asked by an important customer to undertake some awkward jobs. Perhaps they were quite small jobs that were something of a nuisance to produce in a customer's own factory. When this occurred the Abbot, if able, was always glad to help. For example, strip gumming was indeed a sticky operation for the general printer to handle, but not for the Abbot, as it had a purpose built machine. Designed and built by their engineering department, this machine made light of such work and produced a good reliable job.

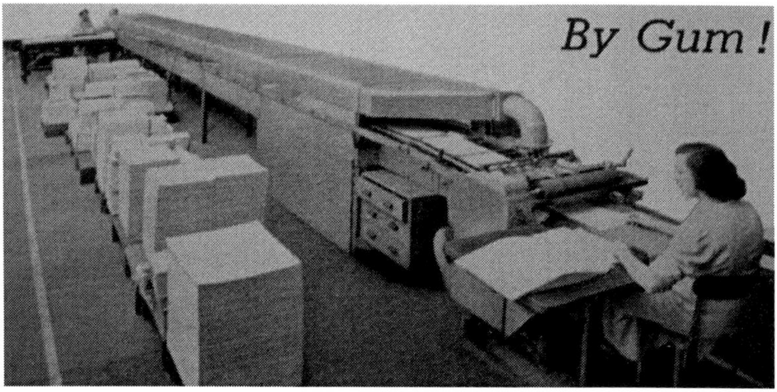

For hot-wax carbonising, this special machine applied a deposit of hot-wax carbon on the back of forms in patches of any desired size and shape, positioned to coincide with the printing on the front. This allowed selective copies to be made, as the carbon was deposited only on the part or parts of a form on which a copy was to be made and not all over. Correct heating and cooling of the liquid wax were vital. Many of the books and sets of forms that the Abbot manufactured had this feature.

The Abbot's plant included rotary and semi-rotary presses. Most of them could handle only one or two webs, but some shown in the picture are three web presses designed for longer jobs that were very often complicated. (Web printing refers to the printing on a continuous roll of paper or an alternative, rather than printing on individual sheets as a sheet-fed press). These machines printed on one or both sides of three webs with a maximum of four colours on one side. The finished job could be numbered, perforated vertically and horizontally, punched, folded and collated. These machines ran at high speeds that were possible only on these reel-fed presses.

The two-colour semi-rotary machines produced cash receipt books. The safety tint in colour, the type matter in black, the perforations down and across, and the numbering on originals and duplicates were all produced simultaneously. They handled strip-gummed or carbonised webs. Exact synchronisation of the various mechanisms was vital, which meant that absolute accuracy had to be maintained both in building of the machines and in setting them up. A constant supply of the same type of work, produced in groups, was the answer to the low production costs that the machines achieved. By their use, even small orders, when grouped with others, were produced economically.

Three web presses.
Machine operators: Edgar Spall & Tom Coster.

Carbon-copy sets, comprised as many as ten leaves of varying sizes, printed to register and often interleaved with one-time carbon paper, were produced. These sets had to be collated by hand, a process requiring great skill, much time and training.

The collated sets were placed in automatic joggers and were then ready for gluing.

The picture (below) shows a row of combined operation machines. These sheet-fed machines simultaneously numbered, perforated, and collated, thereby eliminating the intermediate process of knocking up by hand, which otherwise would have to be done between these operations if this were performed separately. They were capable of handling special jobs in a great variety of styles and sizes and were well suited for the production of carbon-copy sets, pads and stationery for machine accounting systems. This enabled the Abbot to offer the ever prompt and reliable service of work, which, by reason of specification or size, might not have always lent itself to production on the reel fed machines. The last of these machines was taken out of service in March of 2012.

Good business was to be had in the Abbot's duplicate invoice books. These were printed on the remarkable semi-rotary machines. The eleventh machine shown in the picture right was also designed and built at the Abbot. It was one of those that produced the Abbot TD8/FC line. In the picture, adjusting the machine, is Len Ellis, behind him is George Peters. Both worked for the engineering department.

George Peters & Len Ellis

Substantial additions were also made to the Ludlow equipment – which was a hot metal typesetting system used in letterpress printing. The system used moulds, known as matrices or mats, which were handset into a special composing stick. This system cast bars, or slugs, of type out of metal primarily consisting of lead. Those slugs were used for the actual printing and then melted down and reused. Six Ludlow casters, three mono-type super casters and a Nebitype caster, were added. Many new matrices were also added to increase still further the already wide choices of typefaces held by the company. Over 1,000 jobs were set every week, and every one of them was printed from new type.

By the summer of 1953, Eric Freeman had worked 25 years in the Abbot stereotyping department. Eric made this symbolic figure illustrated in the photo taken by Reg Bunyan. Reg worked in the Abbot composing department. This figure was made from two band-saw trimmings from the edges of vulcanised plastic stereos, selected at random from the waste box in Eric's department. He called this so-called work of art the 'Unknown Journey'. Encouraged by the news of a prize of

£4,500 awarded for a similar piece of artwork, he offered his creation to the company for a bargain price of £2,000. Unfortunately, Eric was unable to convince the directors that this would be a good investment. So, he decided to exhibit it in a local exhibition, where it created considerable interest, including a notice in the London press.

After flat-opening binding books became available in January 1953, they were extremely popular with their customers. The thermoplastic replaced the wire-stabbing (stitching) previously used on the Abbot's memo and invoice books. The advantage of these books was that they opened flat and stayed open without having to be held open. If, in the middle of writing an order or an invoice, the customer needed to break off to answer the telephone or a call of nature, the book would not close up. In addition, there was no awkward hump, as with wire-stabbed books. The Abbot soon became inundated with requests for specially printed books that were similarly bound.

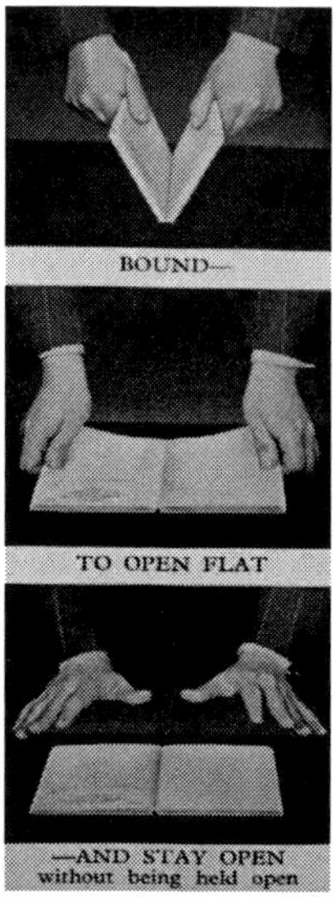

Specialised machinery was necessary for the efficient and economical production of a flexible flat-opening binding. Since fanning out of the work was an important feature of those machines used for thc production of these books, the polyvinyl acetate adhesive penetrated right in between the leaves. Only this process could absolutely assure strength and reliability.

The photocopier probably struck the biggest blow to carbon paper and other early methods of copying, but a new technology was also developed at around the same time with the potential to eliminate carbon paper completely. In 1954 the National Cash Register Company developed No Carbon Required paper (NCR). This process required the pressure of a pen or typewriter

to induce a chemical reaction between different coatings on adjacent sheets of paper. A pen or typewriter produced the original, while the chemical reaction created a blue copy on the subsequent page. NCR was ideal for business forms produced in large quantities, but, in those early days, it was not economical for small applications.

Because the success of the Abbot's business depended on providing for the trade a guaranteed prompt delivery service that could be relied upon year in and year out, a major fire would have been disastrous. Even a small fire confined to one department would have caused a bottleneck that would have disorganised the whole organisation. For many years, the Abbot had a fully trained fire brigade recruited from the staff under the captaincy of Charlie Martin. They were equipped with appliances for dealing with a fire in its early stage. Up until the mid-fifties, a manually operated alarm would sound the works siren and alert members of the works fire brigade. Along with the two night watchmen employed on a regular basis, this seemed to be an adequate safeguard. By 1957, it was thought that the company had grown to such a size that the number of customers affected by any disruption would be catastrophic. Therefore, a Minerva fire detection system was installed, which gave a very early detection of smoke rather than heat. On detecting any smoke in the factory, the automatic alarm not only sounded the factory's klaxons but also informed the Hertfordshire Fire Brigade through a direct link, enabling them to respond quickly to any incident. This became fully operational on July 23, 1958.

Worst-case scenario

Left: Bob Scarborough Middle: Paul English Right: Pete Rolph.

Left: Eric Freeman. Middle: Percy Hunt. Right: Graham Holloway.

Ernie Hill & Charlie Martin.

Left: Archibald Hutchinson
Mr & Mrs Arthur Parkes

Pavitt & Bartlett delivery van. Driven by Bill.

Old Loading Bay.

Abbot No. 1 & No. 2 works 1962.

Gade Engineering Department.

By 1957, help was at hand, as a machine designed and built by the Gade Engineering was brought into service. This collating machine was capable of handling up to five leaves, all the same size. The picture left shows, the machine gathering and cutting off from all five of the zig-zag packs, which are positioned at the rear of the machine. These packs were produced on one of the rotary presses that printed, perforated, punched, and numbered in one operation. This method made for a speedier and more accurate production that saved time and money.

The No. 2 works in Primrose Hill that housed the engineering department, paper stores and patch carbonising departments received a two-storey double bay extension in 1958. This gave the Abbot a much-needed 12,000 square feet (1,110 square meters) of additional floor space.

The 1962 extension to works No. 2.

New machinery was installed in this new extension by the end of 1958. Further extensions were made to the No. 2 works in 1962, which included a canteen, cloakrooms and alterations to the front entrance.

Iva Quelch, is operating the Giebeler machine.

Now that many years have passed since the introduction of thermoplastic flat-opening binding, it is fair to ask if it was a success. From a technical standpoint the answer depends upon who did it and how. Thermoplastic binding was not just a matter of gluing the edges of a number of leaves together with a special adhesive. A job so produced was little if any better than a pad. The adhesive needed to penetrate between the leaves. In 1959, the Abbot had three such machines, each capable of this thermoplastic flat-opening binding process.

In 1959, Print and Print workers, were working a 43½ hour week. However, their unions, NGA and NATSOPA, were asking for a reduction in the working week to forty hours, plus a 10% increase in wages. Employer groups flatly rejected this request and later made an unacceptably low offer of a 2½% increase in wages and a reduction to 42½ hours. A national printers strike began in June that year that lasted six weeks. The printers' unions became the first group of manual workers to achieve a 40-hour working week; however, the 10% increase asked for was drastically reduced. The unions went on to secure a 37½-hour week across the whole printing industry in 1980 and five weeks of annual holiday in 1986. The printing and paper industries were one of the few sectors in manufacturing whose members were covered by national pay and conditions agreements, with employers' organisations across the UK.

Mrs Haysman

At the end of the fifties, many of the Abbot's smaller customers would have liked to use continuous stationery but were put off by the necessity of buying and fitting to their typewriter some form of fixture or attachment or incurring the even greater expense of installing a special purpose billing machine. This changed however, when continuous stationery printed on NCR paper (no carbon required) could be used on any typewriter without any kind of mechanical modification. The customer could simply stand the pack behind the typewriter, feed in and tear off. This was simplicity itself.

The picture of Mrs M Haysman, shows her in 1960. She joined the Abbot in 1930 and had a fine record of thirty years of loyal service. In the picture, Mrs Haysman is operating a drilling machine, but she could operate every type of machine in the bindery department. At that time she was one of the Abbot's most efficient and popular people. The drilling machine shown in the picture is the Soag automatic paper drill, which was installed to drill filing holes, in all types of duplicate books, pads and sets. It automatically drilled holes of various diameters to a pre-set spacing and was installed to meet the ever-increasing demand for business stationery used by customers' filing systems in the sixties.

To commemorate Mrs Haysman's thirty years of service, the company printed an article in the Printers Prophet, the Abbot House Magazine. The *Printers Prophet* was first published in 1925 and appeared regularly three to five times a year, with the exception of the war period, when the paper controller had other ideas. It was the aim of the magazine to keep in touch regularly – though not so regularly as to become boring – with those who sold the goods that the Abbot manufactured.

Horace Luckett, who joined the Abbot as a boy of 16 in 1927, was appointed a director of the company on August 1, 1964. Working his way up through the estimating, order, progress and costing departments, he gained a very wide knowledge of the company's business. He became an office manager in 1946. Horace was one of the original players on the Abbot football team during the early thirties.

Horace Luckett

Ira Bartlett always encouraged a friendly atmosphere amongst his workforce. On returning from their annual leave his staff brought him photographs of their holidays, which Ira, added to the large photo album kept on his bookshelf. One of these pictures was of Horace Luckett and his wife in Cornwall. Kings Langley is 296 miles from Land's End, or so it said on the signpost when this picture was taken of the happy holidaymakers in 1965. In the photograph, Horace is all smiles, but this could change on his return from his holiday as he was largely responsible to decide what the prices of Abbot's specially printed listed lines should be.

Mr & Mrs Luckett

In 1964, Arthur D. Parkes retired from the board after forty years of service with the company. He was responsible for buying all materials. He did much to gain and retain the goodwill of the Abbot's suppliers. He was thanked for his splendid service to the company and wished, along with his wife, a long and happy retirement. At the same time, Harold H. Oliver, manager of the order department and Leslie J. Baker, manager of the estimating department, were appointed directors of the company. Harold and Leslie joined the Abbot on the same day in 1931. Leslie, an ex-navy man, was known as the 'Admiral'.

Harold H. Oliver
Appointed

Arthur D. Parkes
Retired

Leslie J. Baker
Appointed

Over the years a local barber, Mr Midgeley from Chiperfield, attended the factory every Wednesday and cut hair for a nominal fee of 1/3d (6¼p), the price in 1949. Brylcreem was always included in the price. Appointments were booked by entering your name against a time in Mr Midgeley's appointment book. Then on your chosen time, you would go along for your haircut – in the company's time of course.

Until May of 1963, the Abbot's service in continuous stationery had, with some exceptions, been confined to small and medium-sized jobs. This changed with the installation of a fine new rotary plant, which ran sweetly and smoothly at quite astonishingly high speeds. It handled those long and very long runs quickly and economically. By the mid-sixties, the Abbot works was set up to produce an array of different printing jobs. Many of the machines used for these jobs were designed and built in the Abbot's very own engineering department.

Six generations of one family have worked for the Abbot. Considering the time that the Abbot has been in existence, this remarkable record at first would seem unlikely, but it is true. The first member of the family was Champion Swift of Sunny Court, a beautiful prize winning German Schnauzer dog, whose great-great-great granddaughter, Champion Zanerush Beauty, became a member of the Abbot workforce in 1968. The two loyal canine employees and each of their relations in between accompanied Percy Ridgley on his duties as chief night watchman. Little wonder why the works was never burgled during their reign. Percy, who retired in 1968, bred them all. He was also an official judge for the Kennel Club. Following Percy's retirement, Zanerush Beauty continued patrolling the premises at night. In August of 1954, a large number of intruders were reported in the factory. Following this, staff were asked not to leave food of any kind lying about, as this would help prevent further invasions of these mice.

Zanerush Beauty

Swift of Sunny

Late one Sunday night in 1969, an anonymous telephone call was received at Hemel Hempstead police station. The caller reported that an explosion would occur at 10 a.m. the next morning at the Abbot Printing Works, Kings Langley. That

Sunday night and at daylight the next morning, the premises were searched by police officers. But nothing was found. On the arrival of the office and works staff in the morning, all were ushered into the canteen; the situation was then explained to them. Due to the factory layout and the many places where explosives could have been hidden, they were asked to inspect their normal place of work to see if anything had been disturbed over the weekend. After a reluctant search by the staff, it was reported that nothing looked suspicious. Nevertheless, it was decided that the premises should be evacuated between 9.40 and 10.30 a.m. A one-way traffic system was put into operation outside of the factory. Few of the four hundred factory workers and office staff were particularly concerned about the possibility that an explosion would actually occur as most took up a view on the grass verge across the road from the main factory. Canteen workers in bright coloured overalls sipped soft drinks and were laughing and joking, as they watched the police struggle to keep the traffic flowing. The only good thing to come of this non-incident was that the staff spent some time in the warm sunshine; not long enough to get a nice tan but it was a welcome break. Normal production resumed thirty minutes after the explosion deadline.

Staff returning after the hoax.

The topic of conversation among the staff was the reason why the hoaxer would pick on their factory. Most agreed that it would be difficult to find anyone with a grudge against the company. Nobody could remember having heard of anyone being sacked or of any recent trade disputes that caused any unrest. It was more likely it was just someone being – banging out, of order.

By 1970, the use of computers had grown rapidly, which had led to an increased demand for continuous stationery. Much of the office work, previously handled by loose forms or pads, were now being addressed with this more efficient stationery. Continuous stationery was a little more expensive to use, but this did not lessen its demand. The extra cost was more than offset by the savings of time by using this type of stationery. As a result of these advantages, many printers were being increasingly asked for this type of work. Fortunately, unlike many other printers, the Abbot had the plant necessary to produce very nearly all kinds of continuous stationery.

Two price increases were forced upon the Abbot in 1970. Whether this was the blame of Harold Wilson's unpopular Labour government or the incoming Conservative party led by Edward Heath was difficult to tell. The fact remained that two complete sets of price lists and catalogues had to be printed and circulated in less than twelve months. A further set of catalogues needed to be printed and circulated before Monday, 15 February 1971, to take into account the change to decimalisation – pounds, shillings and pence were replaced by today's system of 100 pence in the pound.

By the mid-seventies, a second gumming machine was added to the Abbot's many and varied collection. This new machine built by the Gade engineers, was for the application and drying of gum strips on the first leaves of the Abbot receipt books. The method was to apply strips of gum on reels of paper, which were guided on a web through a heated channel on a journey high into the roof of the factory to dry before returning for the rewind. This enabled the company to produce all of the listed lines of Abbot specially printed receipt books on automatic presses. These presses printed in two colours, numbered, perforated down and across and also collated with duplicated leaves – all ready for binding. Their customers definitely preferred receipt books with strip gumming to those gummed all over.

Gumming Machine

A second-hand Giebeler machine was also purchased, along with a Zig-Zagger printer from Timsons. This 24 inch fixed cylinder stationery machine cost £11,000. Mr Oliver and Mr Barker had been looking into the possibility that the company might make its own boxes or cartons. Purchasing these items was costing £15,000 per year. It was agreed that the manufacture of these boxes would be cheaper, and a second-hand machine was purchased in 1975. Annamarie Gibson operated this machine. A second machine was later purchased and operated by Annamarie's granddaughter.

Due to the retirement of Tom Wainwright, the rotary department manager, in September 1977, it was necessary to make changes to some of the departmental managers at the No. 2 works. Vic Lythaby assumed the overall responsibility for both the continuous and rotary departments. Tom Coster continued to be directly responsible for the rotary under Vic Lythaby. Robert (Bob) Cowley trained to be Tom Coster's deputy when required. The responsibility for the hand-finishing and machine-finishing sections situated at the No. 2 works remained with Elsie Surridge and Dick Waterton, although Vic Lythaby oversaw both of those departments. Elsie became the kingpin of the hand-finishing department. She was a strong and fiercely loyal member of the team. Feared by some, but with a heart of gold, she acted as 'auntie' to many of the female staff as well as being their Manager.

The company continued to tick over during the seventies, as there was little space available for any further expansion. However, the printing industry was also seeing many of the traditional ways of producing its products changing rapidly during this period. Large investments would have been necessary to stay ahead of their competitors.

Bielomatik.

The Social Side

The company always promoted a relaxed and friendly atmosphere. It encouraged and looked upon the staff as family. As early as 1924, the company formed a social club and held annual social dances in the Church House, Church Lane, Kings Langley. These types of evenings had become very popular during the twenties. They were exuberant and energetic events. In between the dancing, games and competitions were organised. Never missing an opportunity, Ira Bartlett wrote in the back of the 1925 programme: 'To our visitors, see what nice girls we have at Pavitt and Bartlett. We want twelve more nice girls, like these to join our happy family; we will be pleased to receive applications at the works'.

In 1946, the Abbot social club acquired the use of a clubhouse, which was situated alongside the lake opposite the main factory. The company owned this land, but at the time the Kings Langley Angling Club was using the lake. Formerly a gravel pit, the lake was flooded in 1922.

During the excavation of this pit, remains of prehistoric animals were found, and between the war years a German bomb fell and exploded in the lake. Many Abbot employees used the facilities of this clubhouse, which had a well-stocked bar. Other facilities in the clubhouse included a piano, dartboard, billiard table, card room and a television lounge upstairs. Before long a darts team was formed, which played in the Watford Business House League. The players included Eddie Price, Tom Coster, Pete Weedon, Fred Taylor and Colin Lowe.

By the late 1920s, the annual dance had moved from being held in the Church House, to the Abbot factory. All of the tables, chairs and equipment were removed to make room for these spectacular occasions. They were always enjoyed and well supported. The picture above shows, the 1928 festivities in full swing.

It was rumoured the TV lounge in the clubhouse was being used by some couples, not for flicking through the limited number of channels – ITV would not start broadcasting until 1955 – but for more flirtatious purposes… Other facilities included four boats for sailing on the lake. Reg Bunyan and Eric Freeman each owned one of these boats. There was also a terrace, where on summer days, people could sit overlooking the lake while enjoying a drink. An area was cordoned off for swimming and diving. Brian Bartlett enjoyed taking his daughter, Dinah, with him when he swam in this lake.

The Clubhouse. & Terrace.

Clubhouse Bar: Harold Oliver & Mrs Wright.

Unfortunately, the company suffered considerable loss owing to the default of the social club secretary. It was hoped that when the club was re-organised, it would be able support itself, but this proved not to be the case. The takings of the club had become insufficient to cover the day-to-day operating costs, even though the company provided the premises and certain other services free of charge. Interest in the club had also begun to diminish. Therefore, the directors of the company decided that it was no longer worthwhile for the company to bear a continued loss, and the clubhouse and facilities were closed in December of, 1951.

Sailing on the lake.

During the 1950/51 football season, the Abbot employees arranged a charity football match in aid of a sick colleague, Peter Weedon, who was suffering from Tuberculosis (TB). The match played at Home Park Mills was between two works teams, the Upstairs Wanderers and the Downstairs Rangers. All of the proceeds went to Peter and his family.

The Downstairs Rangers team players were Tom Coster, Tom Knight, Horace Luckett, Bernard Timberlake, George Chandler, George Russell, Mike Dunham, Bill Majors, Ronnie Rogan, Bill

Crudess and Eddie Chalk. Playing for the Upstairs Wanderers were Brian Latchford, Ron Funnell, Dennis Hopkins, Des Bryant, Vic Lythaby, Bill Reeves, Pete Burgin, Ray Clift, Pete Plestead, Pete Holloway and Peter Rolph.

There can be no output without some input. The following pictures of the Abbot canteen and kitchen show where a lot of the input was prepared and served.

About half of the workforce stayed for lunch, at which three courses were served daily. There were ten-minute tea breaks in the morning and afternoon. Management felt that it was better for the workers to spend time away from their normal place of work and to take a few minutes for a cuppa and a cigarette.

As the canteen was not large enough to hold everybody, the breaks were arranged at staggered intervals on a departmental basis. A meal was also served for the regular night shift. From April 1948, Nurse Carroll was the supervisor of the canteen until September, 1951, when Nurse Randall took over this responsibility. Elsie Surridge, who had taken over the hand-finishing department in 1950, later took over the responsibility of the canteen.

A committee, formed from the staff, administrated the canteen. They were always congratulated on a really high standard of quality and service. For the regular diners, there was always a free Christmas dinner. It was noticeable each year that the number of regular diners slowly increased during the weeks leading up to this free Christmas dinner.

Adjoining the canteen was a snooker room, in which snooker was played with a varying degree of skill. Anybody who wanted to win a bob (5 pence) or two need only challenge one of the directors to a quick game. One of the snooker tables was moved into the No. 2 factory in the late 1970s. The second table was then sold, and the proceeds went toward the refurbishment of the remaining table.

In addition to the dances held in the factory, another very important event was the children's Christmas party, at which was performed a pantomime written and directed by Reginald Bunyan. These were always produced on nearly a professional level, although this was sometimes debatable. The cast for these pantomimes were chosen from Abbotonians, and the children always enjoyed these productions.

Jack and the Beanstalk Pantomime 1950s

Other attractions at the Christmas party included Tom & Jerry cartoon films – probably the same ones were shown every year. There was also an array of stalls, games and sideshows. Another popular attraction was the miniature railway, which was set up on the factory floor. The children were given a tour of the factory while riding on this train. Ira and Peter Bartlett would take turns sitting up front driving the train. Brian liked to dress up as a ticket collector and would show the young passengers to their seats. It was questionable who had more fun, the children or the Bartlett's.

Peter Bartlett driving with Dinah Bartlett behind him. (1949)

Some of the children enjoying the Abbot Christmas Pantomime 1950s.

Before the arrival of Santa with his presents for the children, all their little tummies would be filled with an endless supply of jelly and ice cream. Happy Days!

Rock & roll and free love conspired to produce fashion that would last well beyond this decade of the swinging sixties. Mary Quant set hemlines and many a young Abbotonian men's temperature soaring, with the miniskirt... In the first half of the sixties – for women's fashion – the look of the late fifties remained. Stiletto-style heels were still very popular with the women in the early sixties, but not so popular with the Abbot's management, as the heels would continually cut up the office carpets. The miniskirt

became more popular in the second half of the decade. Most women took a while to accept this new look. For the mini to work, the old-fashioned underwear and stockings of the fifties had to go. Women now wore tights. With this decline of stockings and suspenders, young male Abbotonians had to find something new to fantasise about. The rise of hemlines seven to eight inches (18 – 20 cm) above the knee did help to compensate! Some of the younger Abbot males of the time adopted the Mod gear – a smart suit with narrow lapels and tapered trousers, with a slim tie and winklepicker shoes.

Also during the sixties – possibly to take their minds of these rising hemlines – an Abbot Cricket team was formed. The team played the majority of its games against different departments at the John Dickinson Paper Mill in Apsley. Other employees got together and started two ten pin bowling teams, The Abbot Monks and The Abbot Friars, which played against local firms in the area, mostly on Tuesday evenings. The company paid for some team T-shirts with the Abbot trademark printed on them. They competed in the 'Saints and Sinners Cup' with a varied degree of success. Some of the players on these bowling teams included: Tom Coster, Mick Reynolds, Tom Wainwright, Bob Scarborough and Jack Parrott. During the sixties and seventies, Abbotonians enjoyed many coach trips, which included seaside trips to Margate and weekends in Blackpool.

35-Year Club

Employees who had worked for the company for 35 years became members of the Abbot's exclusive '35 Club'. In recognition of 35 years of service, they were awarded a gold watch at a presentation held in November each year. The earlier gold watches were engraved on the back with the words 'Abbot (Kings Langley) Ltd', followed by the dates and the individual's name. Later, the watches were presented in a case with the wording engraved on a plaque on the lid. Members of the '35 Club' were entitled to attend the annual meeting, to an extra day's holiday, and to the privilege of not having to 'clock in' for work.

The club was formed in 1963, but the 35 years were counted from November of 1923, when the company first started trading from Kings Langley. That first year, 22 members of the staff qualified, including, of course, the three founding directors. A decade later, in 1973, the club presented Ira Bartlett with a small-engraved cup to commemorate 50 years in Kings Langley. Horace Luckett made a speech at that meeting. A copy of his hand written notes follows:

"This is the eleventh meeting of 'The 35 Club', but there is, of course, something rather special about today for, as you know, it is the 50th anniversary of the opening of this factory. It was felt by a number of members - with Mr Vic Lythaby the leading light - that we could not let this occasion pass un-noticed.

"Now I am not much of a hand at public speaking, and I hope you will bear with me if I have to consult my notes pretty frequently. I will be quite honest and tell you that, when I was asked to do this, my first inclination was to wriggle out of it altogether, but it was pointed out that, after our Chairman, I am the longest serving member of the company, so I really had very little option.

"As most of you know, when Mr Bartlett and Mr Hutchinson started this factory 50 years ago, things could not have been much more difficult. There was still considerable depression following the First World War; unemployment was high; there was a lot of unrest amongst the working population, which culminated in the general strike of 1926. Money was very tight and it must have taken a lot of courage to 'go it alone'.

"I was not among the '6 men and a boy' with which I understand the factory started, but I can still remember from my early days that the first thing IAB did when he came in each morning was to make a bee-line for the office to enquire how much money had come in that day. No doubt this was to assess the prospects of paying the wages at the end of the week.

"As the years went by and the company progressed, this approach altered somewhat and it was usually Mr Parkes who received the first visit with the query 'Any orders Arthur?' whereas today it is more likely to be the same comment as to the need for a certain building project not far away from where we are now.

"I suppose it would not be difficult to go on for quite a time recalling events of long ago in the early years of struggle - the rapid expansion in the late 1920's and early 1930's - the excitement when a further extension was built or new machinery installed - the upheaval caused by the war and the changes which took place afterwards, but I am reminded here of the three rules laid down by a prominent after dinner speaker for

people in my present position. These three rules were to stand up, to speak up and to shut up.

"Nevertheless, before I conclude I must say that in my opinion, our Chairman is a remarkable man and what he has achieved has not always been fully appreciated. In Mr. Hutchinson he had a very able partner, but it was his determination, his drive and his forethought which were largely responsible for the success of the company and there is no doubt in my mind that all of us here today and a lot of other people besides, owe him a considerable debt of gratitude.

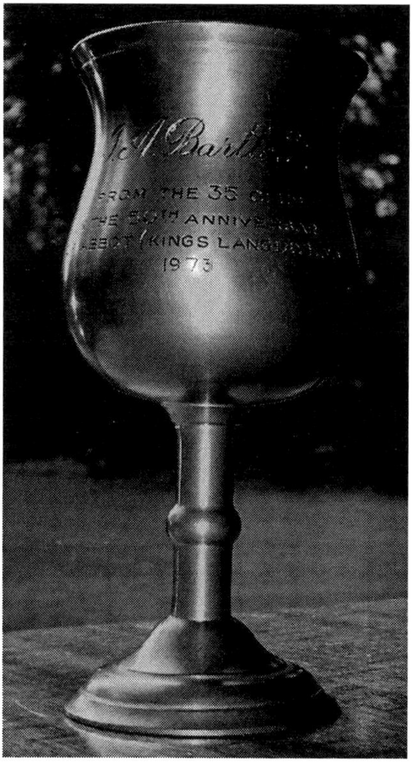

"I estimate he has been actively engaged in business for something like 65 years and although he doesn't come into the office quite so often these days, I can tell you that when he does, he is very much 'on the ball' and keeps the rest of us 'on our toes".

"I am sure I speak for everyone present when I say to our Chairman that we have very great admiration and indeed affection for him and to mark this occasion we ask him to receive a token of our esteem and with it go our best wishes for his continued good health and the hope that he will enjoy 'may a sip' from the goblet which on your behalf I now ask him to accept."

There were a total of 108 presentations made by the '35 Club', during the company's existence. A full list of all those who received these presentations follows:

	Name	Date joined	Other brief details and position at retirement/leaving.
1	I.A. Bartlett	1923	Ira Albro Bartlett, company founder, Chairman. Known as 'IAB'. Died June 16, 1985.
2	A.T. Hutchinson	1923	Archibald Thomas Hutchinson. Also, known as 'ATH' or Hutch. One of first directors. Died 1969.
3	M.E. Woodrow (Mrs)	1923	Secretary to the Directors
4	A.D. Parkes	1924	Arthur or 'ADP'. One of first Directors. Retired 1964.
5	C.G. Brigginshaw	1925	Charlie. Compositor. Died 1968.
6	A.E. Dollimore	1926	Albert Edward. (Known as Bert). Compositor. Died 1982
7	H.W. Dennett	1926	Harry William. Retired 1966. Died 1974.
8	R.E. Freeman	1926	
9	J. Hill	1926	
10	H.W. Luckett	1927	Horace. Director. Retired 1977.
11	C.C. Martin	1927	Charlie. Retired 1977. Died 1991.
12	D. Sayell	1927	Dan. Retired 1976
13	E.F. Spall	1927	Edgar. Rotary machine minder. Union official F.O.C. retired 1977.

14	L.J. Storrow	1927	Les.
15	R. Warton	1927	Ron. Machine minder. Retired 1981. Died 1992.
16	R.C. Waterton	1927	Richard Charles. (Dick). Numbering department. Retired 1981. Died 1994.
17	S.C. Whitby	1927	Sidney. Known as Jock. Foundry manager. Retired 1977. Deceased.
18	E.W. Freeman	1928	Eric. Big chap with a big personality. Retired 1979. Now deceased.
19	R.A. Gurney	1928	Reg. Machine minder. Retired 1977. Deceased.
20	E.A. Price	1928	Edmund Arthur. Known as Eddie. Director of Gade Engineering and shareholder. Died in a car accident, in 1966.
21	W.H. Tipton	1928	Bill. Known as 'Tippy'. Works manager. Retired 1973. Deceased.
22	T.R. Wainwright	1928	Tom. Rotary department manager. Retired 1977. Died 1994.
23	L.H. Channells	1929	Ken. Compositor. Retired 1980. Died 1994.
24	J.G. Parrott	1929	Jack. Rotary machine minder.
25	F.C. Reeve	1929	Fred. Retired 1968. Died 1980
26	P.J. White	1929	Pat. Compositor now deceased.
27	B.I. Bartlett	1930	Brian Ira son of the founder. Known as Mr Brian. MD and Chairman. Retired 1986. Died November 13, 1992.

28	A. Culverhouse	1930	Arthur. Guillotine operator. Union official F.O.C. Retired 1978. Died 1980.
29	W.T. Day	1930	Tom. Compositor. Retired 1978 Died 1981.
30	M. Haysman (Mrs)	1930	Bindery department. Retired. Died 1987.
31	H. Reynolds	1930	Harry. Night shift rotary department manager. Retired 1981. Died 1988.
32	R. Turner	1930	Guillotine operator. Retired.
33	L.J. Baker	1931	Leslie Joseph. Ex navy, known as 'The Admiral' to some. Became a director then, MD when Brian Bartlett retired in 1985. Died 1994.
34	S.W. Brigginshaw	1931	Sid. Compositor. Retired 1978. Died 1989.
35	H.H. Oliver	1931	Harold. Director. Retired 1982, now deceased. His son, David, worked in the office for a while.
36	H.A. Reeves	1931	Harry. Compositor. Deceased.
37	D.C. Sears	1931	Don. Flat-press department manager. Left 1981 now dcceased.
38	H.G. Smith	1931	Gordon, Sales director. Retired 1977.
39	W. Baugh	1931	Walter. Estimator. Now deceased.
40	F.W. Reynolds	1932	Frank. Flat-press manager after Gerry Storrow. Retired 1989. Deceased.
41	F.V. Lythaby	1933	Vic. Machine minder. Retired 1984.

42	G. Storrow	1933	Gerry. Flat-press manager. Retired 1983.
43	R.V. Bunyan	1934	Reg. Worked in the origination department. Was a keen photographer. Sadly lost his sight through diabetes, retrained as a telephonist. Retired early. Died 1980.
44	D. Dwight	1935	Den. Watchman and driver. Lived in a house alongside the factory that was owned by the company. He retired 1981. His wife continued to live there until her death over 20 years later. Den died in 1991.
45	G. Hoar	1934	Gordon. Foreman in composing department. Worked on the night shift continually through choice. Voluntary redundancy 1983. Now deceased.
46	C.S. Bull	1935	Charlie. Flat-press machine minder. Retired 1978. Died 1990
47	L. Grover	1935	Les. Reel-fed department foreman. Retired 1985.
48	P. Hunt	1935	Percy. Foundry. Now deceased.
49	P. Smith	1935	Retired. Now deceased.
50	L.A. Stevenson	1935	Leonard Arthur Stevenson. He was a director and the company secretary. Retired 1973.
51	E. Hill	1953	Ernie. (Previously 1929 – 1946) Compositor. Was a

			despatch rider during the war, was injured during this time. Retired 1980.
52	H. Holloway	1936	Harry. Machine minder. Retired 1974. His son Graham worked in the foundry department.
53	J. Mallord (Miss)	1936	Joan. Hand finishing Department. Retired 1982.
54	E. Surridge (Miss)	1936	Elsie. Managed the hand finishing department and the canteen. Retired 1983. Died 1996.
55	E.T. Scott	1937	Eric. Reel-fed machine minder. Retired 1988.
56	A.F. Wood	1949	Arthur. (Previously 1933-42 & 1944-47) finishing department. Retired 1982.
57	P.A. Bartlett	1938	Peter Arthur Bartlett son of the founder. Retired 1986. Died August 1991.
58	T. Coster	1938	Tom. Rotary department manager. Retired 1990. His partner, Kath, also worked from 1955 - 62 & 1965 - to date.
59	L. Ellis	1938	Len. Gade Engineering Co. Forman. His Son, Phil, also worked for the Abbot.
60	R.C. Mellish	1938	Ron. Director. Retired 1986. Deceased.
61	V. Cowley (Miss)	1940	Deceased.
62	A. Nutkins	1940	Alan. His wife, Doreen, also worked for Abbot. His son Ian was a baker and took a van round various companies at lunchtime. His Lardy

			cakes were something special and were responsible for the expanding waistline of many an Abbotonian! Retired 1990. Died 1997.
63	P. Weedon	1940	Pete. Now deceased.
64	R.F. Beddall	1941	Ron. Director and company secretary. Retired 1986.
65	C. Lowe	1941	Colin. Machine minder. Had been disabled since birth, but still outrun most of the others. Voluntary redundancy 1983.
66	J.G. Rodgers	1942	Jack. Compositor. Made redundant 1986.
67	E.J. Fuller (Miss)	1946	(and previously 1942 - 44) Retired.
68	H.P. Burgin	1974	Pete. (and previously 1944 - 73) Rotary machine minder. Retired 1983
69	B. Turnbull (Mrs)	1945	Barbara. Maiden name Elton. Retired 1991.
70	W.M. Hickey (Miss)	1946	(previously 1943 - 44) Retired 1984.
71	R.Culverhouse (Miss)	1947	Rose. (special on retirement after 34½ years)
72	D. Drewell	1946	Den. Flat-press assistant manager. Made redundant 1986.
73	P. Hodges	1946	Pete. Compositor. His wife Audrey worked for the company 1962 - 94. Made redundant 1986. Died 2013.
74	J. Lawley	1946	Joe. Finishing and packing.
75	M. Saunders (Mrs)	1947	Margaret. Finishing. Retired 1988.
76	R.C. Scarborough	1947	Bob. Foundry department.

77	P.G. Rolph	1948	Pete. Foundry department. Moved to New Forest after his retirement.
78	R.G. Cowley	1949	Bob. Retired 1992. Deceased.
79	C.J. Hearn	1950	Cecil John, but known as John. Sales director. Retired 1990. Deceased.
80	R.W. Landry	1950	Reg. Accounts department. Retired 1991
81	B.G. Mundy	1950	Brian. Estimator. Office manager. Was an active member of the Round Table. Retired 1998. Now deceased.
82	T. Fuller	1951	Trevor. Paper warehouse manager.
83	G. Hales	1951	Graham. Finishing department.
84	J. Chandler	1951	Jeff. Finishing department. Left in 1988.
85	D.J. Bastin	1952	David, known as Diddy. Deceased.
86	G.E. Latchford	1953	Graham. Left 1990.
87	B. Twigg (Miss)	1953	Barbara. Fishing department. Retired 1998.
88	A.J. Weedon	1953	Alan. Started as a compositor, became Managing Director. Retired 1995.
89	W.J. Airs	1954	Bill. Worked in the office. Was a volunteer in the Scout Movement. Retired 1991.
90	J. Baynes	1955	John. Director. Pension Scheme Trustee. Started as a compositor.
91	M. Chandler	1955	Mick. Guillotine operator.
92	R.C. Thomas	1955	Ray. Rotary machine minder.

			Retired December 2002.
93	K.W. Hunt	1956	Kenneth. Lived in Railway Terrace. Retired 1998.
94	V. Norman (Mrs)	1960	Valerie. Finishing department. Made redundant 1998.
95	M. Cooke	1961	Mick. Machine room manager. Retired March 2010.
96	D.G. Fellowes	1962	Doug. Production manager. Pension Scheme Trustee. Retired 2001.
97	K.A. Pignon	1962	Ken. Estimator.
98	K.F. Redgwell	1962	Ken. Rotary department assistant manager. Ken's son Barry and his wife Pauline, both worked for the Abbot.
99	B. P. Michael	1963	Brian. Reel-fed department.
100	M. Reynolds	1963	Mick. Origination department manager. Pension Scheme Trustee. Took early retirement.
101	D. L. Chaffin (Mrs)	1964	Dinah Louise. Brian Bartlett's daughter. Director of Company. Chair of Pension Scheme Trustees.
102	P. Carter	1965	Phil. Was Steve Cooke's deputy as finishing department manager.
103	A.J. Durrant	1965	Tony. Senior Estimator. Retired.
104	C.D. Butler	1965	Chris. Worked in the foundry.
105	S. Cooke	1966	Steve. Manager of the finishing department.
106	B. Lowe	1966	Brian. Guillotine operator.

107	S. Lacey	1969	Steve. Worked in the accounts department for many years. Company Secretary of 'Abbot Print Ltd'.
108	M. Kwarciany	1970	Mario. Guillotine operator.

In November of 1998, Mick Reynolds was presented with a gold watch when he became the 100th Abbotonian to have been with the company for 35 years or more. His father Harry, (retired 1981), and his uncle Frank, (retired 1989), were also members of the 35 Club. His mother (nee Crawley) and his two other uncles, Jack Reynolds and Charlie Crawley, also worked for the company for many years. The 99th member, Brian Michael, who started a few months before Mick, was also presented with a gold watch.

Watch presented to Peter Weedon in 1975.

The 99th & 100th 35-Year Club Members

Brian Michael (99th)

Mick Reynolds (100th)

The last of those 108 presentations was made to Mario Kwarciany in 2005. They accounted for 3,780 years service, quite an achievement for the size of the company. It should be noted, that the vast majority worked well beyond the 35 years required to receive their recognition with the company. They obviously found their time at the Abbot enjoyable and rewarding. Well done to them all.

The Decline

Ira Albro Bartlett Junior, who founded the company in 1920, said that he wished to resign as Chairman of Abbot (Kings Langley) Limited and as director of the subsidiary companies whilst retaining his directorship of Abbot (Kings Langley) Limited. It was decided to make the following alterations and additions to the Board of Directors from January 1, 1980.

Brian I. Bartlett. Chairman of Abbot (Kings Langley) Limited and Abbot Duplicate Book Company Limited.

Peter A. Bartlett and Leslie J. Baker. Joint Managing Directors of Abbot (Kings Langley) Limited and Abbot Duplicate Book Company Limited.

It was also decided that Cecil J. Hearn, Ron C. Mellish and Nikolas J. Bartlett, who were already directors of Abbot Duplicate Book Company Limited, be made Directors of Abbot (Kings Langley) Limited.

The printing industry was beginning to see some significant technical changes. To survive, they had to move quickly to meet and compete in the computerised, digital world. A new printing industry was needed. Because of this new age, the Abbot experienced a reduced volume of orders during 1980. The possibility of cutting staff numbers became a matter of urgency. Employees above the normal retirement age were considered for redundancy, along with the employees who were not directly involved with production, in particular, the canteen staff. Eventually, in November 1980, it was decided to give notice to thirteen employees, who were older than the normal retirement age. Investments in this new technology were being made, but twenty-seven further redundancies were needed from the factory floor in October 1983. By 1984, plans were going ahead to move all production into the No. 2 works. From the beginning of 1985, necessary equipment was moved into the No. 2 works, which was completed by March of 1986. Although, Tilling Plastics Ltd made an offer for the main factory, this offer was subsequently withdrawn. Other interests in the factory site, were made by developers, and a meeting was set up with Three Rivers District Council to see if planning permission could be obtained for the No. 1 factory and the car park, alongside the lake opposite.

The picture below shows some of the staff from the comps (compositors) and foundry departments before the closure of the main Abbot works. At the time of the photograph, most of the equipment had been removed from both departments. The items being kept were relocated to the No. 2 works in Primrose Hill.

From left to right standing: Phil Ellis, Ron Janes, Roy Lamb, Peter Holloway, James Ellis, Dave Hobbs, John Herbert, Bill Gibbard, Peter Hodges, Peter Rolph, Doug Fellows, Jack Rodgers, Matt Darvill, John Warren, Keith Print, Bob Fisher, Bill Cooke, Gordon Hoar, Paul English, Brian Culverhouse, Clive Shaw, Cleaner?

From left to right kneeling: David Davis, Mick Reynolds, Terry McGee, Alan Lucas, Steve Hudson, Alan Humphries.

On April 3, 1985, Brian and Peter Bartlett reported to the board of directors that, due to the deterioration of his health, their father Ira Bartlett, was unable to attend to the business of the company. Taking into consideration the problems with his sight and hearing, it was impossible for the secretary to obtain a formal resignation. The board agreed with regret that it should deem such a resignation to have been received from that day and act accordingly. Sadly, Ira passed away two months later.

Ira Bartlett

The printing industry witnessed so many innovations from increasing use of hot-metal composition during its experimental stage at the end of the nineteenth century to its virtual extinction through the impact of photo and electronic composition by the late twentieth century. In the letterpress field, vast technical improvements were followed by its almost complete replacement by litho printing. In litho printing, also known as offset printing, an inked image is transferred from a plate to a rubber blanket and then onto a printing surface. All the technical changes dramatically reduced the number of employees required to produce print of the highest standards.

Peter Hodges

By the mid-eighties, Brian Bartlett, who had been suffering with Parkinson's disease for some years, became increasingly aware that he could not continue to work and decided to retire. He resigned his directorship on August 26, 1986. Peter Bartlett decided to retire at the same time as his brother. They contacted John Brian Reed, an associate, who was an entrepreneur in the printing industry. They had met through John's brother, Alec.

Alec Reed was married to Ira Bartlett's stepdaughter, Adrienne Eyre. John Reed was the owner and chairman of Reedbooks Ltd. John B Reed Ltd, Reedform Ltd, and Reedprint Ltd. John was unwilling to buy unless he could obtain more than 50% of the shares. Although Peter and Brian between them owned over 50% of the shares, there were numerous other shareholders. Brian Bartlett had passed over his shares to his daughter, Dinah, and her husband. They were reluctantly persuaded that there was no sensible option but to agree to the sale of their shares. Peter Bartlett's adopted son, Nikolas John Bartlett, was also keen to sell. Nikolas was one of the first trustees of the new Final Salary Pension Scheme when it began in 1978.

The sale of the company to Reedbooks took the form of an option to purchase within two years. This option took place on October 20, 1986, and was conditional upon specific work within the business being undertaken. Pensions had to be provided for Mary Bartlett and Brian Bartlett. Peter Bartlett opted to waive his pension. Under the management of Alan Weedon, Reedbooks invested heavily in electronic typesetting.

The original Abbot building was sold in 1987 to Beechwood Homes, part of the Finlinson Group based at Blue Court, Church

Lane, Kings Langley. The Finlinson Group demolished the building, including the distinctive decorative front, to make way for a large residential park. The company contracted to demolish the No. 1 works received a summons from the County Council for commencing without giving the statutory notice. The maximum fine was then £1000. The company solicitor advised them to plead guilty, to which the company agreed. They then received a £25 fine with £25 costs, which the company paid, along with £300 solicitors fees.

Before – The Abbot main works with the decorative front.

After - This residential park, Lakeview, replaced the Abbot Building.

Nikolas Bartlett had struggled with alcoholism all of his life and found things even more difficult under the new management. Eventually he was dismissed. He filed an unfair dismissal claim in 1990. This went to court, but he lost. The family then bought what was once the 'Yates Convenient Store' in Chipperfield. Nikolas helped to refurbish the premises, but he could not be persuaded to work in the shop. He occasionally wandered off, to dry-out without telling anybody where he was going or why. Following the opening of the store in 1994, he again disappeared. Sadly, Nikolas was found in a hotel room in Muswell Hill, London, where he had suffered a fatal heart attack.

When John Reed was a student of the London College of Printing, he and other students were taken to the Abbot to be shown good printing. Some 40 years later, he bought the company. The Abbot was still producing its traditional lines of duplicate books, various types of forms, and pads, as these lines were still in great demand. Few printers existed with the Abbot's experience, in terms of people and machinery, to handle all of the different types of stationery used by businesses across the country. To maintain a competitive product and stay ahead of the market, more investment had to be made in the latest technology. The investment in another Drent Gazelle press gave the Abbot the extra capacity of 3.6 million forms a month at a fast 200 meters/minute. The press featured IMR (In-mold roller technology) that enabled quick make-ready and reduced downtime and changeover on the shorter runs. The move to electronic forms composition with the Digiform gave The Abbot fast and versatile composition facilities. Added value was also offered with all the design features (round cornering, reversals, degraded screens, tints, etc.) required by the Abbot customers. Under John Reed and his managing director Alan Weedon, the Abbot was changing from its old familiar family ways, but was able to maintain its reputation for expertise and reliability and as one of the most highly regarded trade printers in the country.

Some of the longest serving managers found John Reed, the new owners' practices difficult to accept. Doug Fellows, who had joined the company's composing department straight from school in 1962, and over the years he worked his way up to become a production manager. Doug was an outspoken individual, tackling problems head-on. This had earned him the respect of all managers. Unfortunately, there was a clash of personalities with John Reed and he decided to retire in 2001. John Baynes, who also started as a compositor in 1955, he ended up as a director of the company and also a pension scheme trustee. His knowledge of all the company functions, his achievements in the introduction of new production methods, and his skills in negotiating with suppliers, was a huge asset to the company. However, he too found it unacceptable working with John Reed, he then left and went to work with Peter Mahoney. Peter was originally brought in as an Abbot director soon after John Reed took over, but Peter and John Reed had a falling out, so he also left the company.

Further announcements were made in 1989 that there would be more redundancies. Unfortunately, many of the staff chosen to go had made tremendously valuable contributions to the company. Nevertheless, this restructuring was essential for the future of the Abbot. The hard facts were that the company was incapable of sustaining itself at its present size. Even more redundancies were needed in 2003 and 2006.

Abbot. Primrose Hill works.

Natalie York.

Michael Chandler.

Maxine Carter.

Kevin Culverhouse

Darren Latchford.

Phil Marsh.

Pauline Redgwell.

Phil Carter.

Standing: Steve Freeman, Stuart Marriott, & Chris Cook.
Sitting: Mick Reynolds & Norman Waterton.

Steve Lacey.

In October of 1999, a new Horizon in-line perfect binding system was installed. The system comprised a perfect binder, a cooling conveyor, a three-knife trimmer, hot-melt spine glue with side gluing, a pile cover feeder with scoring and double sheet detection. The Horizon was a compact perfect binder designed for operation by one person with single-sided front operating position for ease and safety of use. Primarily, Phil Carter and Kathleen Gibson ran the machine; it was binding up to 300 books per hour. The old way of binding would take at least two hours for 300 books, followed by another hour for guillotining.

With the gradual decline in turnover of continuous forms and book and pad printing, the value of the company was more in the land it was sitting on than as a trading concern.

By 2002, the owners, Reedbooks, decided they were going to the sell off their share in the Abbot, because the Abbot was no longer profitable. The biggest obstacle was the pension scheme, as this made the company's liabilities more than the assets.

In November of that year, John Reed, took on Alasdair Browne, as chief executive. The short-term intention was to put a stop to the year-on-year losses. The long-term intention was to see if it was a viable company and, if so, move the company off the site so that it could release the equity from the land. Alasdair had no previous experience in the print trade. However, Reedbooks thought that this would be an advantage to the business. Alasdair had previously served as an officer in the army, where he gained a lot of experience in high-pressure situations that required a keen-eye for organisation and discipline. Changing to the print industry presented Alasdair with some new challenges. With his background of making quick decisions in difficult situations, he was soon able to learn the business and to restructure the company. It took four years to sell the site. Meanwhile, John Reed had to deal with the long and expensive legacy of the pension fund associated with the Abbot.

In June of 2006, Alasdair Browne bought the assets, staff and goodwill in a carefully planned management buyout. The Abbot moved its business along the canal to Apsley. The name changed to Abbot Print Ltd. The old Abbot (Kings Langley) Ltd existed for a while longer but only as a pension fund and land. The Abbot Duplicate Book Company Ltd was also bought and held (inactive) for future use.

Alasdair Browne

Reedbooks then sold the Kings Langley site to a developer, which developed the land for housing and small factory units. This enabled the pension fund to be topped up and the scheme closed.

Following this buyout, the new director, Alasdair, had the problem of moving to new premises, not something he wants to go through again anytime soon. He said: 'It was not only a case of keeping production going as best as possible, but trying to establish a new building while clearing out the old.' The key element was the staff, which were great. They all pulled together in this changeover period. The Primrose Hill building had almost eighty years of history with various nooks and crannies. Abbot Print Limited is now located just a few miles away at 16 Frogmore Road, Hemel Hempstead, Hertfordshire. About twenty-five people now work for the company. The Abbot still prints business forms, books and pads for trade. It is a smaller, leaner company than it has been in the past, which reflects the relative demand of the products. In recent times, the company has invested in better machines to produce the traditional book and pad work. The aim is that, as long as there is a demand for these products, the name of 'Abbot' will be there to produce them.

This was the end of the Abbot (Kings Langley) Ltd, in the Village. The factory was located in Railway Terrace and Primrose Hill for over eighty years. Ira Bartlett started the business back in 1920 and at onetime boasted a workforce of over 400 people. During its time in Kings Langley, many life-long friendships and relationships were established. No change of location would ever have an effect those affectionate connections...

It is hoped that these few pages of the Abbot's history has provided some insight, of what it was like to be associated with this friendly, family run, printing business, which began its life in the roaring twenties, survived the great depression of the thirties and a world war, to develop into a major local employer only to become the victim of technology.

New Abbot Print.

ABBOT

manufacturers of business stationery, books and pads

Pauline Redgwell.

Kathleen Gibson.

Roy Fuller.

Barry Redgwell.

New Abbot Print.

The Drent Gazelle.

Mick Cooke's retirement, March 2010.

New Abbot Print.

Barry Redgwell, Phill Marsh & Kevin Culverhouse.

New Abbot Print Staff 2013.

Standing: Steve Lacey, Stave Rule, Roy Fuller, Jacci Becket, Phil Marsh, Olive Osler, Jane Greener, Kath Gibson, Sue Wilkins, Sue Waterton, Jane McCauley, Barry Redgwell, Brian Lowe, Phil Carter, Chris Butler.
Kneeling: Ian Carter, Martin Nethercott, Alasdair Browne, Mario Kwarciany, Stuart Marriott, Steve Freeman, Steve Cooke, Chris Cooke, Kevin Culverhouse, Tom Keady.

Abbot (Kings Langley) Ltd

Archibald Hutchinson & Ira Bartlett.

Abbot (Kings Langley) Ltd

Ira with his second wife Mary.

Main entrance before new front was built in 1935.

Abbot (Kings Langley) Ltd

Abbot with the new front.

Charlie Martin - Monotype Caster 1947.

Abbot (Kings Langley) Ltd

Jane (Judy's sister), Peter, Judy & Brian Bartlett.

Abbot (Kings Langley) Ltd

Abbot (Kings Langley) Ltd

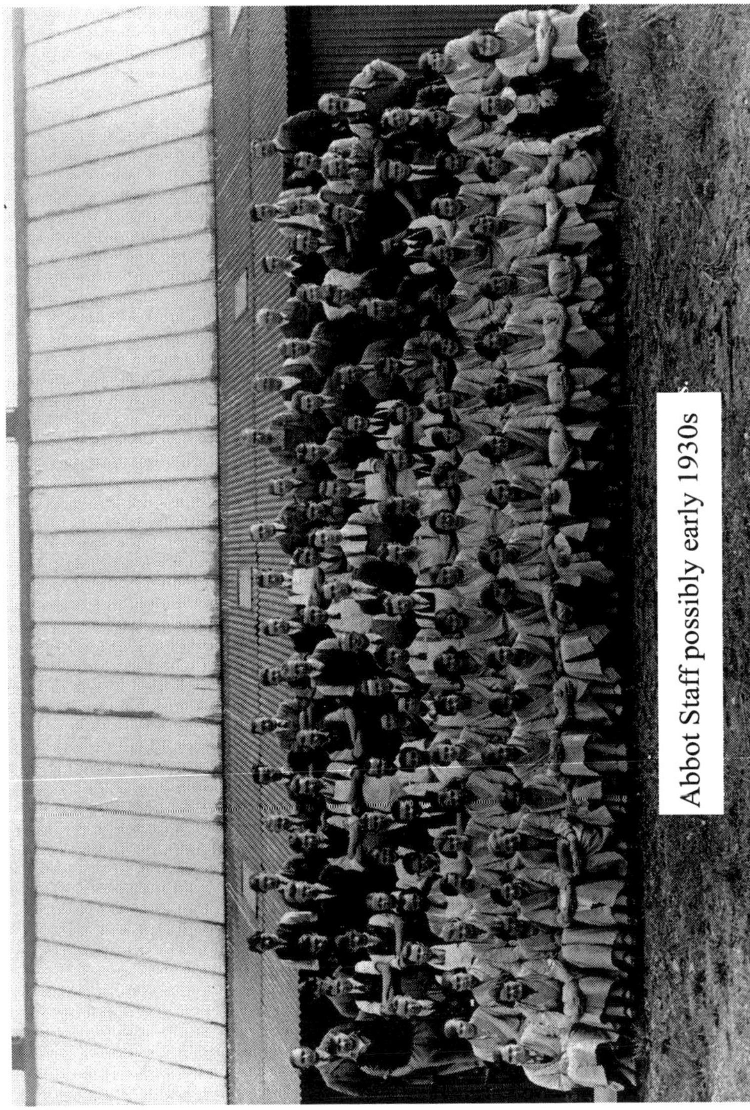

Abbot Staff possibly early 1930s

Parish Boundary 1935

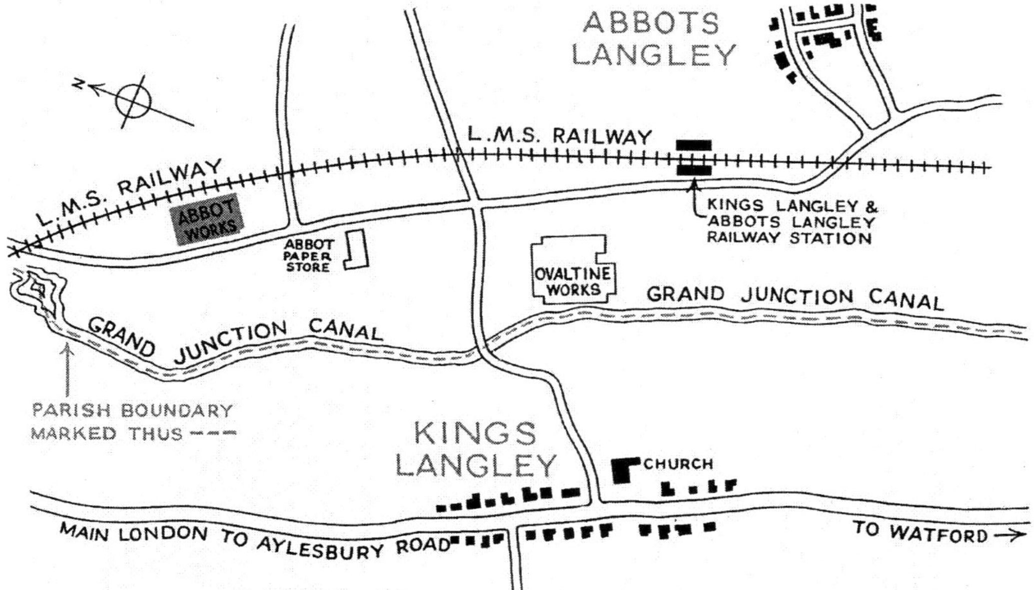

Parish Boundary 1935